SICILY

Originally published in Padova, Italy by Franco Muzzio Editore as

La cucina della sicilia orientale

SICILY *Culinary Crossroads*

GIUSEPPE CORIA

Translated by Gaetano Cipolla

ORONZO EDITIONS

NEW YORK

Italy's
Food
Culture

oronzo editions, LLC
11 West 30th Street
Suite 7R
New York, NY 10001
www.oronzoeditions.com

ISBN 978-0-9797369-3-3
©2008 Oronzo Editions, LLC, English translation
English rights worldwide
Library of Congress control number: 2008937191

Cover: Sicilian oranges

Title page: Taormina coastline

LA CUCINA DELLA SICILIA ORIENTALE
ISBN 88-7021-745-0
©1996 aries—franco muzzio & c. editore spa
Via Makallé 97, 35138 Padova
Tutti i diritti sono riservati
Originally published in Italy
by Franco Muzzio Editore, Padova, Italy.

Italian Series Editor: Marco Guarnaschelli Gotti

Printed in China

Photography credits
Photography copyrights held by the
following.
Cover: Pippa West
RJ Lerich, pages 2/3, 73, 76/77; Joanne
Wruk, 4; Cornel Acherei, 6, 34/38, 74;
Diego Barucco, 12, 22; Ben Shiman,
13; David Lee, 19; Ana Menendez, 28;
Ollirg, 10, 30/31, 80/81, 92, 96/97,
114/115, 116/117, 122, 142/143, 158,
162, 164/165; Bouzou, 39; Juriah
Mosin, 43; Mikael Damkier, 32; Nathan
Kresge, 35; Richard Thornton, 59;
Nathan B. Dappen, 62; Kerrey Mazzey,
78; Aiok, 80; Matka Wariatka, 82;
Danilo Ascione, 88; Sebastian Duda,
99; Deborah Reny, 102; June Maria
Sobrito, 107; Akva, 120/121, 157;
Hamiza Bakirci, 122; Guy Erwood, 127;
Paddington, 134; Gratien Jonxis, 137;
Elena Eliseva, 140; Sandy Maya Matzen,
160/161, 165; Charlotte Moss, 167;
Irina Tischenko, 168, 202; Slava, 201;
Klaus Kreiger, 203; Heather Hood, 205;
Lori Sparkla, 207

contents

SICILY: *Culinary Crossroads* by Giuseppe Coria is part of Oronzo Editions' series of regional Italian cookbooks published by Franco Muzzio Editore and now translated into English. Each book presents hundreds of recipes culled from diverse sources—treasured family notebooks, historical records, elaborate recipe books from the libraries of nobility, and, when possible, personal interviews.

Famed Italian gastronomist Marco Guarnaschelli Gotti, editor of the original Italian series, sought out local cultural experts who became "gastronomic anthropologists," researching centuries-old histories and traditions. Honoring the legacy of Pellegrino Artusi, they emphasize the importance of home cookery in the development of Italian cuisine. And, in the style of Artusi, their writing is conversational, intimate, and opinionated. Their mission is clear—to bring to their Italian readers an understanding of regional history and tradition and, as Coria tells us, to document *exemplary* examples of their regional gastronomy.

Giuseppe Coria, gastronome, folklorist, vintner, and author of ten cookbooks—including *Profumi di Sicilia,* a comprehensive guide to Sicily's culinary tradition—has provided us with this wonderful collection of the island's most important and treasured recipes. Coria dedicated his life to exploring and documenting Sicily's culinary and cultural history. An ambassador for Sicily's wines, he was the first to bottle the celebrated DOCG *Cerasuola di Vittoria* at his Ragusan winery Villa Fontane, encouraged by wine and food critic Luigi Veronelli. As Coria makes clear in his comprehensive introduction, any study of Sicily is not a simple affair. Thousands of years of foreign dominations, overlapping and intertwined, have produced a Sicilian culture, language, and gastronomy that is unique, rich and complex.

Although his study concentrates on four regions well-known for superb cuisine, Coria has documented classic and "rescued" recipes across the island and shown the gastronomic interrelationships of Sicily's nine provinces. He has researched, unravelled, and brilliantly presented Sicily's past for us through the gaze of a gastronome. As you read these pages you will come to see that his gaze is wide—and extraordinary.

—*Polly Franchini, Publisher*

Left: detail of Messina's bell tower

A Gastronomic Map

Sicily's provinces, cities, and towns referenced in recipes

Ustica

Tyrrhenian Sea

San Fratello·

Erice· **TRAPANI**
·Partinico
·Monreale **PALERMO**
·Cefalù
Pettineo
·Mistretta
Castelbuono·
·Capizzi

Egadi Islands

·Sperlinga
·Nicosia

·Marsala

Leonforte·

·Castelvetrano

·Mazara del Vallo
·Sambuca di sicilia

●**ENNA**

·Sciacca

●**CALTANISSETTA**

·Ribera

·Aidone
Piazza Armerina·

●**AGRIGENTO**

·Nisceni

·Licata

Mediterranean Sea

·Gela

Acate·
·Comiso
Vittoria·

Scoglitti·

Santa Croce Camerina·
Donnaluca

Pantelleria

Stromboli

Aeolian Islands

Lipari

MESSINA

Barcellona ·Milazzo

so ·Patti ·Castroreale Terme

CALABRIA

Strait of Messina

·San Piero Patti
·Ucria
·Montalbano Elicona
·Roccalumera

·Randazzo ·Taormina
·Castiglione di Sicilia

·Bronte Mount Etna ·Riposto
·Mascali
·Milo
·Zafferana Etnea

rano·
Pedara· ·Acireale
·Saint Alfio
Belpasso· ·Mascalucia
·Paternò ·Acitrezza

CATANIA

Ionian Sea

·Palagonia ·Lentini
·Carlentini
·Militello Val di Catania ·Augusta
·Francofonte

·Vizzini ·Melilli
·Monterosso
Floridia
·Giarratana ·Palazzolo Acreide SIRACUSA
Chiaramonte Gulfi ·Canicattini Bagni

RAGUSA ·Avola
·Noto
·Modica

·Rosolini
·Ispica ·Marzamemi
·Pozzallo ·Vindicari
·Pachino

GENERALLY people skip prefaces and go the heart of the matter. This, however, is much more than a preface. It is the key to understanding Sicilian cuisine. You cannot enter the island's gastronomy and understand its significance and scope without it.

In any book on regional gastronomy the reader quickly sees that the author is anxious to exalt the specialties of his region, either praising their originality or the balance in their ingredients or the special techniques involved. Naturally, in reviewing the broad and complex panorama of the cuisine of the nine Sicilian provinces, I, too, may give in to some chauvinism, but substantial differences do exist. Nevertheless, my praise will never trespass into useless glorification, nor will I forget to document, black on white, the cases where I underline a recipe's originality or point of origin.

Finally, I remind the reader that this is not a book in which "typical Sicilian" recipes are collected. Indeed, their number has been reduced on purpose to include only those recipes that are *exemplary,* those above all that must be rescued from neglect, forgetfulness, or oblivion.

The rescue operation of these simple ancient dishes of our heritage is now being undertaken in Sicily, both by families and restaurants.

—*Giuseppe Coria*

INTRODUCTION *Culinary Crossroads*

IN ITS LONG HISTORY, Sicily has experienced eleven periods of foreign domination that, superimposed on the indigenous culture of its first inhabitants and establishing roots over time, have produced cultural sedimentations and stratifications that, rather than dispersing the island's social and cultural patrimony, have enriched it, creating the Sicilian people. Sicilians are not a distinct people because they belong to a different race—that is, a group of people who share genetic, biological, and physiological similarities. They are a people because they share customs and traditions that have produced a historical memory which is, in fact, the distinctive factor that makes a people. We intend to look for this memory, placing it in a historical context painted with broad strokes and limited, naturally, to its gastronomic aspect.

Mt. Etna

THE CYCLOPS

Mythology has it that the Cyclops, or the Giants, appeared on Sicilian soil after the Great Flood. Homer[1] described them and all the ancient historians spoke of them. Here, we are mainly interested in pointing out that the Cyclops Polyphemus, who held Ulysses and his companions captive in his cave, ate cheese and drank wine. This is the first occasion in which cheese and wine enter human history, and as chance would have it, Sicily is named as the first location.

THE GREEKS

The Greeks, cramped in their own land, sought new areas for expansion and began colonizing Sicily in the 7th century BC. They landed first at Naxos in 735 BC and from there gradually founded various cities, some of which have since disappeared (Megara, Hyblea, Selinunte, Himera, Kamarina) while others flourish to this day that bear traces of that ancient epoch: Siracusa, Naxos, Zancle (Messina), Agrigento, and many others. Naturally, the Greeks brought with them not only their arms and belongings, but also their traditions, customs, and language. Given the length of their stay, over five hundred years, many words and various customs were

1. The Cyclops were the smiths of Vulcan who made the lightning bolts for Zeus, according to the ancient legend recorded by Homer in his *Iliad*. They had their shop on the slopes of Mount Etna. According to the same legend they were the first inhabitants of Sicily. They were gigantic, so much so that they were also known as *gigante*. They were even mentioned in *Genesis* as children born out of the union between angels and the daughters of Adam. They had only one eye in the middle of their foreheads— the name derives, in fact from *kyklos* (circle) and *òp, opòs,* (eye). According to the Homeric tale, the rocks in front of Acitrezza were the boulders that Poliphemus, blinded by pain in his only eye, hurled against the fleeing Ulysses.

Ancient grave sites

assimilated by the Sicilians. To this very day—particularly in dialect forms—etymology leaves no doubt as to the origins of many words. For example *pitrusinu,* as parsley is called in Sicilian, has almost the same sound as the Greek word *petrosélinon*.

Some forms of worship originally introduced to the island by the Greeks were adopted by the Sicilians. In fact, the myth of Demeter (later to become Ceres in Roman mythology), goddess of grain and bread, would be recorded later by Ovid[2] and by Cicero himself.[3]

It must be said that Sicily remained Greek even during the Roman domination that followed, especially in the eastern part of the island.

Yet external gastronomic influences traceable to the Greeks were limited. The Greek colonizers did know about bread, focaccia, and roast meat, but this applies only to the Athenians, as we can't forget the infamous "black broth," or "slop" of the Spartans. At that time, it was Sicily instead who would export its gastronomy.

2. Ovid, *Metamorphosis.*

3. Cicero, *Tusculanae.*

4. Horace, a Roman poet who lived between 65 BC and AD 8. His most important work was the *Odes*.

5. Plato, *De Republica*, III Dialogue.

6. Epicharmus was born in Siracusa in 485 BC. Son of Titiro or Chimaro, he was Pythagoras' disciple. A comic poet and an excellent philosopher, he was a very learned man who authored many commentaries on the nature of things and medicine.

THE GOLDEN AGE OF SICILIAN GASTRONOMY

From the beginning of the 5th century BC, Siracusa, Agrigento, and Gela were the birthplaces of the finest cooks, famous everywhere under the collective name *siculi coqui*—celebrated in antiquity for the sumptuousness of their tables, the sophistication of their cooking, and the art of their banquet preparations and communal meals.

That fame would endure throughout the centuries, so much so that Horace[4] and other famous Latin authors would write about it. Plato[5] went so far as to say of the people of Agrigento: . . . *Aedificant semper Agrigentini tanquam semper victuri, convivantur tanquam semper morituri . . .* ("They always build as if they expect to live for eternity; they always eat as if they expect to die the next day").

It is worthwhile to remember the figures that made Sicily famous. The first whose name has survived is Epicharmus of Siracusa.[6] In fragments of his comic play *Le Nozze di Ebe* ("The Wedding of Ebe") that have survived, one is surprised to read about "the very tasty fish from the sea of Siracusa" and about the optimal season in which to eat them. He also described a soup containing every species of crustacean. In his other works as well, he took pleasure in gastronomic descriptions. In *Sirene* ("The Sirens"), he related how these sweet creatures nurtured Ulysses not with song but with grilled anchovies, roast suckling pig, young squid accompanied by a superb wine for lunch, and then with fat mullet, bowfin fillets, and scorpion fish for dinner.

Charmo of Siracusa[7] was a contemporary of Epicharmus. He was an eccentric character who became very famous as a poet because he described in rhyme and verse each dish that was brought to the table. Another personality was Panfilo,[8] who became equally famous because when he sat at the dinner table he talked only in verse.

In ancient Siracusa, where a formidable school of the art of cooking flourished (the first "hotel school" we have heard of), the Sicilian Labdaco[9] became the most renowned teacher of his time. The Greeks sent young men to him to receive instruction. Whenever they needed assistance in recruiting chefs to bring back to Greece, they went to him.

The first author of a cookbook was Terpsione,[10] another Siracusan. He created a school of his own in which he gave public lessons on how to set a table, how to serve, and which foods to use and which to avoid (because they were harmful or lacked taste). He was, in short, a precursor of nutritional science.

More important than Terpsione was Mithecus,[11] also from Siracusa, and who in Greece was described as "famous in the culinary arts as Phydias was in sculpture." We know of him also through Massimo Tirio[12] who said of him:

> . . . there went to Sparta a Sophist from Siracusa, . . . the art of this Sophist consisted in teaching what was most pleasurable in our daily needs: in fact, he was able to prepare the food he served at his banquets in such a delicious manner, using a great variety of appropriate condiments, that he coaxed the maximum flavor out of ingredients, going beyond their normal tastes.

The narrative of Tirio continued, recounting that Mithecus was turned away by the city magistrate with the famous words "Sparta does not find food enticing, only work." He was received by other Greek cities with great honor.

As recorded by Giulio Polluce,[13] two other famous Sicilians, masters of cooking, lived in the 3rd century BC: the two Heraclides. One was defined as "Doctor in the art of cooking." The other was also a culinary writer from whose writings we gather many facts about the customs of his time. He described the various types of fish

7. In the *Descrizione della Sicilia* by Giulio Filoteo Omodei (in the *Biblioteca storica e letteraria di Sicilia*) this is how he was described: "Charmo of Siracusa, a very amusing poet who, as Ateneo wrote, was accustomed to conjure up quickly a witty remark or an amusing phrase about any food that was brought to the table." The *Biblioteca storica e letteraria,* ed. by G. Di Marzo (Forni Anastatic edition, 1973–74) covers the historical period from 1600 to 1800. It consists of diaries and numerous unpublished manuscripts by famous authors providing us with very detailed information.

8. Panfilo, a character whose name was passed on to us by Ateneo (see note 14).

9. Labdaco, a character whose name was passed on to us by Ateneo (see note 14).

10. Terpsione lived during the time of Dionysius II (circa 340 BC). He was the author of *Gastrologia* and was apparently a teacher of Archestratus.

11. He wrote about gastronomy in the *De siculorum arte coquinaria (The Culinary Art of the Sicilians), Biblioteca Siciliana,* vol. 2). Plato in his *Gorgias* confirmed this when, on introducing Socrates, he said, "Thearion, Mithecus and Sarampo were healers of bodies who knew how to prepare bread, the first one, food, the second and wine, the third."

View of temple ruins at Agrigento

and for each the best method of preparation; he provided detailed information on the taste of different kinds of eggs according to the type of fowl (in his opinion, peacock eggs were the most desirable); and he described a particular square-shaped bread that was meant to be eaten with olive oil, wine vinegar, and cheese. He mentioned a certain sweet made with honey and sesame seeds in the shape of the female pubis (called *mylli* or *mylloi*) that was consumed during the Festival of Demeter. This was confirmed also by Ateneo,[14] who related: "Heraclides of Siracusa . . . says that in the closing day of the *Tesmoforie*, the feasts in honor of Demeter, they prepared sweets in the form of a pubis that were called *mylloi* all over Sicily and were carried around for the goddess."

But the already long list of illustrious names in the art of gastronomy pales before the figure of Archestratus. Born in Gela, he wrote a volume circa 330 BC, the title of which is uncertain—perhaps *Hedypatheia* or *Gastrologia*—from which (through Ateneo) some sixty fragments have survived, approximately three hundred thirty-two lines.[15] The format followed by Archestratus—almost a "guide to good cooking"—includes for every food listed: its seasonality; the best region in which to obtain it; and finally the best recipe for its preparation. Unlike the opulence and sophistication of food preparation practices popular in Sicily at the time, Archestratus provided precise instruction and a clear approach—the cook should practice *la cucina naturale*, avoiding excessive use of condiments and additional ingredients that mask the natural flavor of ingredients.

At this time, tuna roe caught near Pachino was well-known and appreciated; so were baby suckling pigs raised in Siracusa (salami, sausage, prosciutto, and other types of sausages were renowned for their great taste), and the cheeses from Agrigento were excellent. The honey from the Iblei Mountains near Ragusa was unsurpassed, while pigeon, duck, sparrow, lark, quail, and most of all skylark (a species of quail, still considered a table delicacy) were the most refined morsels in Sicily.

So what remains of the period of Greek colonization? Very little,

12. Massimo Tirio was a Greek rhetorician who lived midway through the 2nd century. He authored forty-one dissertations and left us a great deal of information on the journeys he took to Syria and among the Arabs.

13. Giulio Polluce, a Greek grammarian and rhetorician, lived at the same time as Marcus Aurelius and authored, among other works, the *Onomasticon*, a volume that provided us with much information on ancient times.

14. An Egyptian gastronome and rhetorician who lived in the 2nd to 3rd centuries AD, Ateneo wrote the *Deipnosophistes* ("The Wise Men or Sophists at a Banquet") in which he imagined a gathering of these erudite men who discuss several subjects. It is a precious source for the indirect description of the customs of the time and for the citation of numerous ancient works and their authors, many of which have not survived.

15. The fragments of Archestratus' work came down to us through the work of Ateneo (see note 14). They were translated and published in a little volume entitled *I frammenti della gastronomia di Archestrato* by Domenico Scinà in Palermo in 1823.

I believe, since it was Sicily that exported its gastronomy. Perhaps preserved olives and salted ricotta; certainly the great varieties of bread, given that the Greeks produced over seventy-two different kinds (according to Ateneo who mentioned one particular type, *collùra,* in the shape of a doughnut, a kind of edible toy given to children, which still today bears the name of *cudduredda* on the island, and serves the same purpose); perhaps the practice of adding either milk, oil, herbs, or spices to flour according to the kind of bread desired; and finally, perhaps the use of an oven to bake bread, whose model has remained unchanged through the centuries and is still used in the Sicilian countryside.

THE ROMANS

After the Greeks were driven out during the 1st century BC, the Romans chose to remain on Sicily, a rich and blessed island, and it became under Augustus the first Province of Rome. The Romans remained there until AD 307.

Unlike the Golden Age of the Greeks, the Romans exploited the island as a colony. Governors, consuls, magistrates and functionaries afforded themselves opulent lifestyles, while the general population, deprived of any resources and impoverished, was restricted to frugal meals.

This is the period in which the great divide emerges between the gourmet opulence at the Roman table *(cucina ricci)* and the peasant's menu *(cucina povera)* based mainly on vegetables, some gathered from the wild, and other products from the land. Because Sicily was the "granary of Rome," the local people had access to bread, which, fortunately, was never lacking. A kind of bread called *cudduruni* (the first pizza) was born. It consisted of dough that was flattened for rapid cooking and eaten before bed for the sole purpose of having something in one's stomach to keep hunger pangs at bay.

This period coincided with the decline of Sicilian cities. The agricultural economy was burdened by the creation of large agricultural estates, barely offset by an increase in the breeding of horses and other animals, the production of wool, the fishing industry, and the extraction of minerals.

The names of cities changed: Akragas became Girgentum. Zancle became Messana, whose port began to decline slowly. Tauromenium (Taormina) began to develop and became an excellent wine producer; Panormus (Palermo) became the main port for the export of wheat to Rome; Siracusa survived as well as it could while continuously losing inhabitants.

In terms of gastronomy, the Romans left few traces. Focaccia, or different kinds of small breads, now called 'mpanate by Sicilians, indicated anything cooked "in bread" —a term which unfortunately many writers have derived from the Spanish *empanadilla,* forgetting that this word was inherited by the Spaniards from the common language spoken in Rome. Cato even gave us the actual recipes for some of these focaccia: the *placenta* for example, which is made with flour, cheese, and honey from the Iblei Mountains, a classic recipe of the time recorded by Martial;[16] and the recipe for *mustaceos*, which would become the pasta *mostaccioli*.[17]

The Romans also helped us to appreciate asparagus. It grows wild all over the island even today; they gave us an appreciation of snails; made us understand that wild hare was the best meat (although Sicily was always a rich source of this kind of game); and that it was better to cook the skylark stuffed inside an onion shell. They taught us—and this practice is something the Sicilians have never forgotten—to eat only fresh meat and cook it well, never to age it; to store snow in caves for use in the summer; to make better use of tuna fishing facilities; and "to cook liver in nets" (see Siracusa section).

It was perhaps during the Roman era that many species of fruit trees were first introduced to the island. They had been brought to Rome first by the Roman generals returning from their conquests in Eastern empires. Thus the cherry tree, to cite one example, was brought by Lucullus[18] after his victory over Mithridates.

On the other hand, Romans discovered artichokes on Sicily—as recorded by Pliny[19]—tasting them there for the first time, as well as other local specialties, including the honey from the Iblei Mountains near Ragusa.

Franks, Goths, and the Byzantine Empire

The first signs of the decline of the Roman Empire, sealed by the split between the Eastern and Western Empires, were felt through the unopposed incursions into the island by the Franks (a group emerging from the unification of many different tribes on the left bank of the Rhine, from where they were infiltrating the empire). In 280 they captured and sacked Siracusa.

The Goths, a powerful tribe from the Baltic region that fought and defeated the Romans and were encouraged by their victories, began to mount pirate raids that pushed as far as the coasts of Greece

16. Martial lived between AD 40 and 102. He was a poet who wrote satirical epigrams which often contain references to the gastronomic life of his time. See for example Epigram V, 39 (*Epigrammata*, Pezzano: Venezia, 1716.)

17. In his *De agricoltura*, Marcus Portius Cato (who lived between 234 and 149 BC) gave indications, among other things, on the healthy and simple life and thus he discussed at length a few recipes that should be good and healthy at the same time. One of these involved an early version of our modern *mostaccioli*.

18. More than as a Roman general, Lucullus was better known for the famous banquets and dinners he offered to his guests. As for the cherry tree, it seems that he brought one back from Cerasonta, a Greek city of Asia Minor, the present day Kiresun, already kown for having received Xenophon and his ten thousand soldiers. The Romans called Cerasonta *cerasus*, hence they applied the same name to the tree.

19. The artichoke became widely known to the Romans. Columella appreciated it and Varro recommended grinding the seeds of the artichoke in water and laurel to obtain a taste similar to the artichoke.

and Sicily, plundering several Sicilian coastal cities and leaving them in ruins. The Goths never established a presence on the island, which remained under the control of Roman estate owners.

It is certain that these peoples—nomads, predators, and warriors—always hungry for food and, tied to their own traditions, gave nothing and took nothing from the Sicilian tradition. Considering that Sicilians were as averse to giving or taking as the invaders, we can reasonably conclude that no culinary osmosis occurred among these groups for over two hundred years.

Justinian, Emperor of the Eastern Empire (527–565) embarked on his ephemeral dream to reconstitute the Roman Empire. As part of his overall tactics to achieve this, he sent troops into Sicily under Belisarius. The Byzantines took control of the island in 535, and they held it for about three hundred years, that is, until 827.

During this period, only the Byzantine Empire was effectively in dominance. In this time span—the Middle Ages—we know that meat was cooked on large spits and the consumption of spicy cheeses was very great. The custom of cooking cheese to the melting point goes back to this time (perhaps this is the origin of the famous *caciu all'argintera*), and the use of sour milk and eggs as binding agents in recipes, as well as food itself.

In pastry making—not developed as yet—we note the use of certain biscuits flavored with honey, including those that were first boiled in water before being baked in the oven, *viscotta scaurati* (scalded biscuits), prepared in this manner even today. The use of certain words such as *stigghiola*[20] for example, can be credited to this long period of time.

"THE ARAB GARDEN"

In AD 827, after several previous incursions, the Arabs of the African coast mounted the conquest of the island. The first city taken was *Mazar* (now Mazara del Vallo), then *Mars Allah* (the "City of Allah," Marsala). Then in time Palermo fell to the Saracens in 831, Messina in 843, and Enna in 849. They pushed all the way to Siracusa in 878 and Taormina in 902. This date marks the moment in which all of Sicily effectively fell under Arab control.

The conquering Arabs were cultured, well-educated, efficient administrators and entrepreneurs. The idea of subjugating the Sicilians was never entertained, rather the objective was to integrate them into Arab culture. In Palermo alone—the administrative and military center of Arabian Sicily—over 200 mosques arose, the port intensified lucrative commercial activity, and art, culture and agriculture flourished.

20. The term *stigghiola* derives from the ancient *stihhl*, pole, and by extension "on the spit." In fact this typical specialty consists of little entrails around stalks of onions and cooked on embers. (The following words also can be traced to this period: *arinca*, herring, from *hareng*; *gisieri*, meaty ventricle of chickens and birds, from *ghisieri*; and *sfritu*, *sfidu*, waste, the stuff that is lost.)

It is from this phenomenal place that new things began to radiate to Europe: Arabic numerals, those we use today; the art of distillation; the introduction of new trees (they planted the first citrus groves and introduced the cultivation of sugar cane,[21] rice,[22] and cotton; the first orchards of pomegranates and pistachios; the increase of fruit crops such as peaches and apricots; innovations in cultivation; the introduction of madder, for example, used as coloring agent in the dyeing industry, and the spectacular art of silk production and tapestries by skilled craftsmen.

They passed on the art of drying figs and grapes; introduced exotic spices from the East such as camphor, mace, musk, amber (which has since fallen out of use), saffron, cardamom, and cinnamon (which have remained part of traditional cooking).

Sicily— "The Arab Garden"—was divided into "three valleys," or three departments: *Val Di Noto, Val Demone,* and *Val di Mazara,* a subdivision that would have been wise to maintain over time as it better represented the regional divisions and homogeneity of various local ethnicities. However, these "Valleys" absorbed Arab influence to different degrees. The areas around Trapani and Palermo were greatly influenced by the Arabs; in the central area the influence diminished somewhat, and it was least felt in the eastern area of Sicily.

Many of the sweets that so pleased the rulers and the ruled are of Arab origin, as we see when we review the recipes: for example *le crespelle di riso col miele, cassata, sorbetti,* marzipan, *cubbaita, nucàtuli, sfingi,* and a series of indulgent treats that were enjoyed equally by both groups. Sufficient to say that *lukum,* small chewy sweets available in the Middle East and in Italy today, have the same etymological root as certain Sicilian dialect words currently in use, such as *liccu* (greedy) and *liccumie* (sweets for gluttons).

THIS must be said—not only in regard to the Arab influence—that gastronomic influences were not merely adopted wholesale by the Sicilians, but were modified according to their tastes, their particular needs, and almost always were enriched and perfected. The Sicilians enhanced the cooking of rice by creating a ball that was then stuffed

21. Michele Amari is the author of the monumental *History of the Muslim in Sicily,* written in the 1850s. He provided documentation according to which the first cultivation of sugar in Europe occurred in Sicily thanks to the Arabs. There were sugar cane plantations everywhere. A diploma from 1176 recalls the existence of various mills for sugar cane operating in that period (see Rocco Pirro, *Sicilia sacra,* 1733). This activity continued even more intensely until the 15th century, but it declined in the 16th century when sugar from Brazil and particularly from the Canary Islands became available. But the cultivation of sugar cane never stopped completely. Suffice it to think that the military airport of Comiso, in the Ragusa area, was built in a zone that is called *cannamelito* (sugar cane field) and that the town of Trappeto in the Palermo area owes its name to the *trappeto,* the mill used for the extraction of molasses. Sugar continued to be produced in this area until the early 1800s.

22. Idrisi is the abbreviated name of the Arab geographer Abu Abdallah Muhammad ibn Muhammad ibn Idrisi (1100–1165) who served King Roger and wrote a work with a title as long as his name: *The delight of those who are fond of traveling around the world.* In the book, among

Mongialino Castle ruins in the Province of Catania

di riso (deep-fried rice balls). In short, the islanders made Cato's motto their own: *discere, non perdiscere* ("learn, do not merely absorb").

THE NORMANS

This is another fortunate period in the history of Sicily. While the rest of Italy was in the hands of the Barbarians (Rome had become a village strewn with enormous piles of rubble), in Sicily, under Robert the Fox and Roger d'Hauteville, we witness the emergence of an embrionic Kingdom of Sicily, 1060–1091.

other things, Idrisi pointed out that rice was cultivated in Sicily in the triangle formed by the towns of Ribera, Sciacca, and Sambuca di Sicilia. This is the first time that rice appeared in Europe. (It was not introduced by Spaniards in the Po Valley in the 16th century, as even many respectable encyclopedias incorrectly state.)

Roger's last direct descendant, Constance, married the Holy Roman Emperor Henry VI; their son and heir, Holy Roman Emperor Frederick II von Hohenstaufen ascended to the throne in 1198. He exhibited an enlightened approach that has rarely been matched before or since. For example, he continued to rely on the skills of the knowledgeable Arab officials and courtiers, many of whom served at his court, and he governed wisely and well, contributing many just laws.

Under his rule, Sicilians began to eat *baccalà* and *pisci stoccu,* salted and smoked cod fish, imported from Northern Europe. (Such products arrived in Spain and Portugal only in the 14th century and only then did they spread everywhere.) Stockfish arrived first in the port of Messina, where its use became so deeply ingrained that even today *stoccu* is one of the main specialties in Messina's gastronomy.

Throughout Italy and Europe, spits over open fires were used to roast meat. In Sicily, as there were no fireplaces due to the climate, a kiln with embers was used (the *fornacella* came into use during the Greek period), a cooking technique that would spread everywhere only after 1200. The cooking at the time was also characterized by the preparation of stews and sauces, not yet known elsewhere. The oven continued to play a large role in food preparation. On wealthy estates, the *seneschal*, professional overseer, and *monsu*, French chef, began to appear.

Finally, this was the period in which nuns and monks began to create in their kitchens the "convent" foods that the culinary tradition of Sicily owes so much.

THE ANGEVINS

The Angevins, who came to power after a bloody struggle with the Swabians, remained in Sicily for a short period lasting only 12 years, fortunately. They were expelled by the famous Sicilian Vespers revolt of 1282.

A few small areas remained "French," as those who did not leave were integrated into pre-existing French settlements. This brings us to mention the Gallo-Italic ethnic minorities that came to Sicily with the arrival of the Normans and the Arabs' departure. The point in speaking of these people is not so much to take note of the fact that their "language," the local dialect, is completely unlike those spoken in any other Sicilian community, or that they have different customs and practices that have endured over time, but rather to account for an atypical cuisine in these areas, one that betrays its different origins.

Here are therefore the names of these "French" cities of Sicily: Nicosia, Sperlinga, Aidone, and Piazza Armerina in the Province of Enna; and San Fratello, San Basilio, Fantina, Fondachelli,and Novara di Sicilia in the Province of Messina.[23]

23. San Fratello for example, rose in the 12th century when Adelaide of Monferrato, the third wife of Roger the Norman, brought down a colony of Lombards. A dialect emerged which, while built around the orignal Lombard base, contains a mixture of linguistic elements from the Monferrato region, of Milanese, French, of Anglo-Saxon roots, and elements of Greek. Analogously, the town of Nicosia which was also formed when the Normans arrived, rose around a group of Gallo-Italic colonists from Piedmont, Lombardy, and Emilia Romagna. In both cities an atypical gastronomy developed. We can document this by mentioning, among other things, special polenta called *picciotta* or *piciocia*, made with peas, fava beans, and chickpeas. Another example is a sausage prepared with pork meat mixed with rabbit, as well as special votive breads known as *rociéte* or *luciette*, prepared even today and distributed after they have been blessed on the occasion of the feast of St. Lucy, whose name they borrow as she is the protectress of "light" and of sight.

Returning to the Angevins, we don't identify any gastronomic innovations in this period. A few terms of obvious French origin remain and are still in use today, for example *ragù, matalòtta, gattò, fricassé, gratté, sanfasò, sciabbò* and so on, names that we will meet in the course of our journey. We hasten to add, however, that in terms of techniques and ingredients for these Sicilian dishes and specialties, the only thing that is French is the name.

THE Aragonese

After the expulsion of the "French", the Aragonese became the next rulers (1282–1410). Under Peter III of Aragon, the Kingdom of Sicily was created. It was another golden period for Sicilian gastronomy, which was enriched with the technique of frying. New techniques emerged, such as the gold coloring of dishes accomplished by spreading egg on them and putting them in ovens; creations by the *monsu;* the invention of refined sweets, such as the *biancumanciari* (white food) which will be known elsewhere as blancmange and with other similar names.

This was also the period when the "convent cuisine" and pastries made by nuns developed. In almost every convent in Palermo, nuns prepared sweets to order for wealthy households (King Martin himself was a habitual client).[24] It was the only source of income the convents had and each one became specialized in the production of a particular sweet that became famous and continued over time: the Convent of the Martorana became famous for the fruits of the same name, prepared with a mixture of almonds and sugar and then placed in sulfur or plaster molds in the shape of fruits. (Such little fruits were served at a dinner prepared for Pope Clement V in 1308.) The Badia Nuova convent made the best *cannoli,* together with *Turks' Heads* and *Cassatelle;* the Convent of Saint Elizabeth made the most delicate *nucatuli* on the island; the Convent of the Conception specialized in making *muscardina,* the so-called *paste forti* (strong pastries) or cinnamon pastries which were extremely popular during the feast of the Patron Saint Rosalia; the Convent of the Virgins created the very famous *fette del Cancelliere* (the Slices of the Chancellor) and Pastries of the Virgins that survive to this day.

These things happened also outside of Palermo, wherever there was a convent. Thus pistachio couscous and marzipan shells (*conghiglie di paste reale* in Italian) were created in the Convent of the Holy Spirit in Agrigento; almond *biscotti* in the Convent of the Benedictine nuns of the SS. Rosary of Palma di Montechiaro and so on. Let's not forget that the non-religious pastry industry began only shortly after the year 1500.

This was the period in which a precise differentiation occurred between the *cucina povera* of peasants and sailors—which fortunately still exists on the island—and the cuisine of the Court, nobility, and professional cooks. We offer the classic example of the well-known *caponata*. It was born in noble or wealthy households. This delicious dish, made with eggplants, tomatoes, and other vegetables, with a sweet and sour sauce, included the addition of fish (normally squid, or slices of some other type of more expensive fish). When it was copied by maids and servants in their more modest kitchens, the *caponata* no longer included fish and that, incidentally, was an improvement in the taste of the whole.

SPANISH DOMINATION

The Spanish domination, which succeeded the Aragonese, lasted nearly three hundred years, from 1421 to 1713, but it will not be remembered with nostalgia. For the record, Spain ruled in a terrible and oppressive manner and unfortunately, piling woes upon woes. Sicily was subjected to disasters, earthquakes, pestilence, and famine during this period.

It's taken for granted that the Spaniards left some traces of their presence in the little field we are surveying. I reiterate, however, that rather the creation of new dishes,[25] it was a matter of providing names or details for certain dishes.

Under the Spaniards, of course, after the discovery of America, new things arrived on the scene: tomatoes, peppers, potatoes, beans, corn, cocoa, vanilla, pineapples, and turkeys. But these foods, at least for the part that concerns us, were developed and prepared in Sicily by Sicilians. Naturally, they represented new foods for everyone, Spain included, and therefore no models existed that one could copy or elaborate.

Perhaps the Spaniards gave us the habit, often excessive, of using saffron and other spices brought to us by the Arabs; the use of onions in *cipollata*; and the habit of frying squash in a sweet and sour sauce which the Palermitans ironically call *ficatu di setti cannola*, "liver with seven tubes." The *Pan di spagna* (sponge cake), used to complete the *cassata*, was certainly imported from Spain. The baroque tendencies typical of the time would inspire Sicilian pastry chefs to enrich the *cassata* and beautify it with multicolored candied fruits.

Two other ethnic groups who settled in Sicily during the 16th century must be

24. King Martin the Young (1374–1409) was the son of Martin I of Aragon. He was married to Maria of Aragon, heiress to the Kingdom of Sicily, and then, in a second marriage, to Bianca of Navarre. In a letter dated February 27, 1401, he ordered the Treasurer of Palermo to acquire the following sweets for his household: *Dudichi rotula di citrata 'oy cucuzzata et quindici di pignolata et venticinqui di mendoli confetti* (a document taken from the volume *Spigolature di vita privata di Re Martino in Sicilia*, G. Beccaria, 1894).

25. Among the dialect terms of Spanish origin still in use today we recall the words *ranza*, a bread made with a mixture of flour and bran (from *granza*); *capuliàtu*, the dried tomato cut as a half moon (from *capolar*); and *sciurnari*, to take out of the oven (from *deshornar*). The following words are of Catalan origin: *criscimugna*, yeast (from *creixmoni*); the verb *amburracciari*, to fry something after dipping it in egg–of Castilian origin (from *emborizzar*); and *picarda*, the *vastedda*, a focaccia or type of bread from *gastel*.

View of a Palermo terrace

mentioned. The first were the Albanians who, following the death of their leader George Castrioti (known as Scanderbeg), began to emigrate in large numbers, creating a diaspora. A large contingent settled south of Palermo, precisely in an area that came to be known as Piana degli Albanesi. Others went to Santa Cristina Gela and Contessa Entellina. They brought along their customs, their language, their patron saints, and arms with which to work. In this area, specific Albanian customs survive to this day and, naturally, ancient remainders of their family cooking traditions are present in their gastronomy.

The second ethnic group was composed of inhabitants from Italy's Campania region. After 1544, when the Turkish pirate Red Beard attacked the Aeolian island Lipari, the Spanish government deemed it wise to repopulate it with colonists from Campania. On the other hand, the island of Ustica, which is barely sixty-five miles from Palermo, was left exposed to pirate incursions from the 14th century to the middle of the 1800s, at which time the Spanish fleet, first, and then the Bourbon's, kept it free from attacks. The island of Ustica was fortified and repopulated by the Bourbons, this time with other contingents of people from Campania, some of whom came from Lipari.

This explains why on these islands there are certain specialties that call to mind their Campanian origins, such as the lobster *alla turrisa,* that is cooked in the manner of Torre del Greco in Campania.

THE BOURBONS

After the Peace of Utrecht (1713), Sicily was ceded to Austria and became part of the Kingdom of the Two Sicilies under the Bourbons.

In the field of gastronomy, the Bourbons, who were hardly refined and who lived almost exclusively in Naples, contributed nothing.

Perhaps on account of the mutual exchanges the famous Neapolitan *Polipi affogati al pignatiello* ("squid drowned in the little pot") could be considered progenitors of our *Polipi na quartara*[26] ("squid in a terracotta jug"). We can't confirm whether the Neapolitan dish was born first or the Sicilian, or if both were created with perfect synchronicity by the creative brains of two different cooks from the Kingdom of the Two Sicilies.

26. These are young squid that in the area of Naples are hermetically sealed inside a terracotta pot after adding various aromatic spices. In Sicily the same technique is used with an earthen jug having a narrow mouth that is normally used for water. The mouth is sealed with gypsum and then placed over embers. Once the squid has been cooked (experience will tell you how long it takes) the jug is broken to release the squid, by then piping hot and deliciously aromatic.

THE SAVOY DYNASTY

The Savoy rulers landed on Sicily in 1866 when Italy was unified. They had been there before for a brief period. At least until 1894 this era was marked by a general worsening of the situation. The economic conditions of the island, instead of improving, worsened to the point that when the people paid taxes, when they bid good-bye to husbands and sons as they left for long military service, and when they felt hunger due to the impoverishment of their land, they cried out with a typical expression—half statement, half question—that became proverbial: *Ma cu passàru i Savoia?* ("But who came through here, the Savoy?")

As this is not a history book, but one on gastronomy, we will refrain from speaking about the woes that the Savoy rulers created, but will limit remarks to the era's gastronomy.

First of all, with the state's expropriation of ecclesiastical properties, many convents and monasteries were forced to close, causing the loss of some of the "glories" of Sicilian gastronomy, especially in pastry making.

Fortunately, some nuns continued to live like nuns outside the convents in private homes. They were called *monache di casa,* home-bound nuns, and taught their art to others so that it would survive. The last *monache di casa* were those from the Convent of San Carlo in Erice who were famous for their *cedrata,* lemon cake, and infused all their creations with the soul of the *cedrata.* Fortunately, these are still prepared in this enchanting city.

The only imports from Piedmont were the *savoiardi,* or at least their name and their unusual shape. This biscuit was, in fact, well-known to Sicilians, first as *Pan di spagna,* imported from the Iberian peninsula, as we saw before, and then with the name of *firringòzza* which was produced locally. Nothing new, therefore.

On the question of *zabaglione,* is it French-Piedmontese or Sicilian? I will let the reader judge.[27]

THE history of Sicilian gastronomy cannot be told in detail for many reasons, but primarily because, after Archestratus, no cookbooks were written that could have documented the ancient customs for future centuries. In the enormous number of ancient works on Sicily, both published and unpublished, and even in the chronicles of the *Biblioteca storica e letteraria*[28] that was published from 1600 to 1800, we can glean information on history, agriculture, botany, zoology, economy, customs, and traditions—but we cannot find a thing on the use of food products, the types of food eaten and least of all on recipes.[29]

To put together this volume on Sicilian gastronomy we rely on oral tradition, on a vast repertory of household recipe books passed on from mother to daughter;[30] on the consultation of a considerable

View of Cefalù's harbor

27. According to Italian linguists the word *zabaglione* derives from the late Latin word *sabaia,* a kind of beer coming from the Illiria regions [now Albania]. The Arabs, however, used the word *zabad* which means "foam produced by water or other things" (see Gioieni). They also use the verbs *sabat* and *sabbat* which mean "to slam, to bang." These will give the Sicilians *zabbìna,* which means "that which forms foam when cooking ricotta;" *zabbòbbia,* which means a liquid food, not solid matter;" and *zabbòfia,* which refers to "an abundant liquid food." Consider that *zabaglione* is a liquid, foamy food that is beaten or frothed, and that its roots are of Arabic origin, that the Arabs came first to Sicily; and finally that sugar, which is used to beat eggs, was available in Sicily first (leaving aside any discussion of Marsala wine). I leave it to others to decide the question of the *zabaglione's* first appearance.

28. See note 7.

29. In a rare case (this time on the occasion of the feast of Saint Rosalia of August 9, 1772) the Marquis of Villabianca made a list of the expenses incurred for this annual solemn event. Not talking about food and gastronomy was part of the culture of the time. Even Michele Amari (*History of*

number of the ancient and modern literary works mentioned before (from which we can squeeze bits of information by deduction or comparison); and finally on my own notes gathered by going through towns and streets, tasting and collecting explanations.

Needless to say, from all this data I have come to the conclusion that a cohesive Sicilian gastronomy does not exist. The variety and the differences between one town and the next, between one area and another, depend on a great number of variables that can be summarized.

First of all, as we have seen, foreign dominations determined a stronger or weaker influence according to their settlements so as to produce a "Greek" Sicily, mostly in the eastern areas, and an "Arabic" Sicily in the western areas. Second, the intermingling of various people coming from other regions or countries (ethnic minorities) was also important, as was the mixing—when a new community was created—of groups of people coming from different towns within Sicily.[31]

Another important factor is the geographic configuration of the island with its rosary of numerous cities strung out along the perimeter; the hinterland cities; and the areas of the plains, the hills, and the mountains that are all characterized with different agricultural economies and therefore with different products and primary ingredients available to them.

Another variable is the climate, with areas that are very hot, others temperate, and others that are cold or extremely cold. It is easy to understand that such differences, by necessity more than by choice, will show in the food they eat.

Finally, social, economic and cultural conditions have a bearing as well, and produced a prevailing *cucina povera* gastronomy, in contrast with the *cucina baronale,* both of which, however, were exceptional, unique and inimitable.

Thus we can say that the cuisine is different from one end of the island to the other. One common factor among Sicilians is that they have always considered food—be it poor or rich, common or rare, expensive or not—not only as physiological nutrition, but as a satisfaction of the sense of taste, or better said, of good taste.

the Muslim in Sicily) after disposing in two short pages of certain *camangiari* (food to eat), more to discuss their etymologies than to describe them) apologized, saying: "... Some people may be shocked that I deal with such trifles, considered unworthy by the historians of past generations ...."

30. In a family recipe book, I found a recipe entitled *Viscòtta mazziàti* (beaten biscuits) with the following ingredients: strong flour one and one-half cup, fifteen eggs plus five yolks, two coffee cups of oil and a little more to beat them. That's all there was. It is an easy recipe for the one who wrote it, but an absolute mystery for future generations. Of course, the verb *mazziari* in Sicilian means to beat up, to pummel, and from this we can deduce that the dough was well-kneaded on a marble table. We can also understand that we are dealing with biscuits and, using our intuition, guess that the biscuits were to be cooked in the oven.

31. The city of Vittoria in the Province of Ragusa is a classic example. It was founded by Vittoria Colonna Henriquez in 1604 to develop a fertile territory that was covered with forests. After the band to populate the area was posted (it included land grants, tax exemptions etc.) colonists came not

only from nearby towns such as Ragusa, Comiso, Chiaramonte Gulfi, Modica, etc. but also from Vizzini and Licodia Eubea. The latter colonists brought along their own customs and practices, and even the patron saints of their original towns, so that each group created its own church in the new town Naturally, the different food habits and characteristics of each group were fused together so that in Vittoria you can find recipes and specialties that document their different origins.

In sum, this food is a symbol that awakens as well complex psychological reactions before, during, and after being ingested to satisfy the innate hedonistic component.

Eat to live, or live to eat are not axioms the islanders adhere to: they eat, of course, to satisfy nutritional needs related to the body, but they live also because through eating they want to satisfy needs of a spiritual nature. This is so even if they are about to eat *pasta con le fave*.

Needs are summed up, fused, balanced, and give life to a gastronomy that is unique for its variety, opulence, color, and smell; a cuisine that is inimitable because of its origin, but most of all because it is primordial for character and continuity. And what matters most is that everyone likes Sicilian cuisine, even foreigners.

nota bene

MOST of the recipes that follow come from a time before modern appliances and tools appeared in the Sicilian domestic kitchen. Ingredient amounts, times and temperatures for food cooked in the family hearth, on the wood-burning stove, or on a spit were entirely up to the knowledgeable cook who, for the most part, passed along her wisdom verbally.

ALTHOUGH our author could well assume his readers knew the basics of Sicilian cookery, those of us who were unfortunately not raised in Sicily may need help. Many of these recipes are so well-known to Sicilian cooks that specifics are not needed; many come from ancient sources with missing elements. So we have added in some recipes ingredient amounts and instructions to help our readers along, hoping to do this without intruding on the intent of the original recipe writers.

AS a rule we do not list food substitutions, as this would diminish the authenticity of the recipes. "Italian" ingredients are becoming more available to the American consumer as the popularity of this cuisine grows. Also note that many unfamiliar ingredients can be found using our Resources page.

—The Publisher

messina AND ITS PROVINCE

Messina's legendary Cola Pesce is considered by many ancient writers as a "marvel of nature." He spent most of his life in the Strait of Messina and, since he could not stay out of the water without suffering, he was nicknamed *pesce,* fish. The legend relates many of his exploits, including how he disappeared. One day King Frederick of Sicily threw a gold cup into the sea twice to test Cola Pesce's swimming abilities and both times he retrieved the cup, but on the third try he never emerged.[1] Messina too, could be called a "fish city" on account of the abundance of fish in its two seas, the Tyrrhenian and Ionian; for the famous swordfish[2] that is caught in the Strait between Scylla and Charybdis,[3] and also for the great variety of fish caught off its shores (some found only here); and finally for the *pisci*

stoccu (smoked cod fish), not found in other provinces, where *baccalà*,[4] salted cod, is eaten instead. Consequently, fish is more prevalent in the gastronomy of this province than in the others and the fish specialties that exist all along the coast are numerous. Messina, in fact, can boast one of the very first, if not the first, breeding of mussels in the Ganzirri bay.[5]

Messina is close by the Peloritani Mountains, the highest mountain chain in Sicily, if you exclude Mount Etna. In these mountains, a different gastronomic culture has existed since ancient times based on cheeses, dairy products, sheep, mushrooms, and vegetables and legumes. It's so unusual that we find a unique specialty here: a pasta dish made with chestnuts. Meat dishes are scarce, but the few that exist have become proverbial, such as the *braciulini a missinisa,* small rolls of meat that have been flattened, stuffed with various ingredients, and then cooked on embers with aromatic herbs.

Messina competes well with all the other provinces with its sweets. The *pignulata* of Messina, one of the most delicate Sicilian sweets, is as famous as its *pisci stoccu.*

Just as it is not easy to distinguish reality from the illusion created by the Fata Morgana,[6] which from time to time left the people of Messina stunned, it is equally difficult to discover the real origins of this city's gastronomy. Think of the port that has seen a continuous mixing of races, uses, and customs for centuries. Think of the two coastlines, which, lacking continuity, are oriented toward the Ionian Sea and Catania on one side, and the Tyrrhenian Sea and Palermo on the other, and feel the influences of the bordering provinces. Think finally of its population, consisting of sailors, peasants, and shepherds. Do not be amazed, therefore, about the surprising variety of dishes that our splendid Messina offers.

1. Many writers of Sicilian history recall the legend of Cola Pesce. Giulio Filoteo Omodei provides us with his version (see page 14, note 7, the *Biblioteca storica e letteraria di Sicilia*):

"Cola Pesce lived at the time of King Fernando of Naples around 1460 of the Christian era. He spent all his time swimming in very deep water so that he acquired almost the same nature as fish. The citizens used to compete to go out on their boats just to see him and his amazing feats. Sometimes he remained under very deep water for an entire day."

2. The best fishing occurs in April, May, and June when the fish are spawning. During the other months, they have no taste. The fishing has been described in every era, but we would like to share the following excerpts from a description by Antonino Mongitore (*Della Sicilia ricercata*):

". . . the fishermen who are involved in this fishing prepare a boat that they call *luntre*, a name derived from the Latin *linter*, meaning ship. They install a twenty palms-high pole in the middle of the boat and they adapt a little wooden board as support for the fisherman who has to climb it to see the fish from high and alert the other men in the boat. The men are armed with a harpoon and a rope one hundred and twenty meters long . . . . The most capable of the fishermen hurls his harpoon when the fish comes within range. The wounded fish begins to flee pulling the rope that slows him down. This slowing is called *coloma*. . . ."

The most remarkable excerpt from Mongitore's description is the following: ". . . the remarkable thing about this fishing occurs when the swordfish approaches the boat. The fishermen invite it by speaking Greek to it, as they believe that the fish does not understand Italian. . . ."

Further along in the text the author reveals the mysterious Greek words he learned from the Messina fishermen:

Mamassu di pajanu.
Paletta di Pajanu.
Majassu di stignela.
Palettu di paenu palé.
Palé la stagneta.
Mancata stigneta.
Pro nastu vardu pressu
  da visu,
  e da terra.

Naturally we will never know what kind of language it was. Surely it was an ancient ritual formula to exorcise the fishing and to ensure capture of the prey.

3. Mythology describes Scylla and Charybdis as two frightening monsters. Scylla was the daughter of Hecate and sister of the enchantress Circe. She had twelve feet and six heads and she devoured sailors. Charybdis, on the other hand, swallowed and regurgitated the boiling waters of the sea three times each day. The legend places them on the extreme points of Sicily and Calabria, facing each other, creating thus the Strait of Messina, which was a location of horrible disasters and dangerous crossings.

4. There is a saying about Messina: "There are three things Messina never lacks: wind, stock fish and bad news." The bad news refers to the terrible earthquakes that have always plagued this city. As for the winds always blowing in Messina because of the currents in the Strait, they are a reference to the ancient myth that located Eolus, "the god of the winds," on the island of Lipari, the same god who gave Ulysses the famous goatskins that helped him sail. The saying, however, may allude to more recent times, and specifically to a certain Don Pietro Malizia who is remembered in Sicilian legend as a man who died and did not go to heaven or hell or to land, but was condemned to wander in the skies of Messina as wind.

5. Ganzirri is a suburb of Messina four miles from the center of town. Since ancient times mussel breeding has been conducted in the horseshoe-shaped bay through the use of perches and structures that guaranteed optimal yields. The calm running water and its mild temperature are ideal conditions for this sort of cultivation.

6. The phenomenon of the Fata Morgana effect is nothing more than a mirage that is typical in the Strait of Messina. It was observed by the Greeks and Romans, and witnessed by Polycletus and Aristotle among many others. It is caused by special effects of refraction and reflection of light rays through layers of air that create an optical illusion so cities and people appear where none exist. The ancients attributed the effect to the enchantress Morgana who was as beautiful as she was powerful. According to the legend she had her residence in the Strait of Messina and caused ships to founder when she made land appear before the unfortunate sailors.

oven-baked pasta

Pasta 'ncasciata

The Sicilian name for this dish means "Pasta in a Chest." It was originally cooked inside a pan that was covered with embers placed on top of the cover, so that the pasta was cooked with heat from above and below. Then it became oven-baked pasta.

Ingredients

1 onion, finely chopped
Extra-virgin olive oil
10 ounces (1 1/4 cups) diced pork
1/4 cup pork rind, roughly chopped
10 ounces (1 1/4 cups) firm, dried sausage, crumbled
2 cloves garlic, finely chopped
1 tablespoon *strattu* (tomato extract) diluted with a little water (see page 83)
3 tablespoons chopped fresh or canned tomato
Sea salt
2 pounds cauliflower, leaves removed
1 pound rigatoni
Caciocavallo, sliced finely
Grated pecorino

For the sauce, heat a little olive oil in a skillet and gently fry half the chopped onion until golden. Add the diced pork, pork rind, sausage, garlic, and tomato extract. Fry, mixing well for a few minutes, then add the chopped tomato and enough water to cover. Cook until the sauce has thickened and add salt to taste.

Bring a large pot of salted water to a boil and blanch the cauliflower until just tender. Then strain (reserving the water for the pasta) and separate into florets. Coat the bottom of a skillet with olive oil and gently fry the cauliflower florets and the remaining onion. Bring the water from the cauliflower to a boil and cook the rigatoni in it until al dente.

Once drained, mix half the pasta with one third of the cauliflower, one third of the sauce, and a few slices of *caciocavallo*. After blending, pour this mixture into an oven-proof casserole (the "chest") and layer on some of the sauce, cauliflower, and cheese. Put the second half of the pasta over these layers and then add the remaining cauliflower, sauce, and *caciocavallo* slices. Top with an abundant amount of grated pecorino. Bake covered in a preheated 350° oven until the cheese has melted and the flavors are combined.

Variation

Some people add fried eggplant and slices of hard-boiled egg between layers.

semolina polenta
Pulénta

An extremely humble dish made with semolina. Extra flavor can be added by substituting meat or vegetable stock for the water. The name pulénta *is typical of Ucria.*

Ingredients
Semolina (durum wheat flour)
Water
Sea salt
Extra-virgin olive oil

Bring the water to a boil and add the semolina slowly in a steady stream, taking care to mix continually to avoid lumps forming. Continue cooking, stirring continually, until the required density is obtained—a shorter time for soft polenta, but at least 8 or 10 minutes for a firmer consistency. After making polenta, you can cut it in slices when cold and then you can fry them.

Variations

If you pour semolina into water used while cooking fennel or brussels sprouts, you will get *arriminata di finucchiddi,* fennel polenta, or *arriminata di cavuliceddi,* brussels sprouts polenta. Add olive oil and complete with red hot pepper.

When we say **polenta** we think of the polenta made in some northern regions with cornmeal. In Sicily, analogous preparations exist as well. These are basically a continuation of the *puls* of the ancient Romans. The only difference is that the main ingredient is durum wheat flour (semolina). A number of specialties are made from this that take various names. It's called *arriminata* in the Palermo area; *simulata* in Roccapalumba; *frascàtula* and *piciòcia,* a very liquid dish, in the areas of Enna and Modica respectively; and *picciòtta,* a very rich dish served in a semiliquid texture in which the flour binds meat and broccoli, in the Province of Enna

To complete the topic of polenta, we add that some are prepared with cracked wheat (but not reduced to flour) with which *farinata* is created in Roccapalumba; and *simuluni* in the Enna area. It's also prepared with *farro,* typical in Sambuca di Sicilia, but with the same name *farru,* and with the name *pitirru* in the Province of Agrigento; with orzo, which gives rise to the *miniscìna d'oriu* in some parts of the Enna area; with chickpea flour, giving rise to the specialties known as *papitacciò* and *cicirata,* typical of the Palermo's province. From couscous we have *milinfanti* and *frascàtula.*

SOUP WITH MEATBALLS AND BROKEN EGGS
Sciusceddu, Sciuscellu, Ciuscello

A traditional Easter dish.

A similar dish is made in the Palermo area, but this dish differs because the little balls are made of meat, and most of all because eggs and ricotta are added to the broth, which makes it similar to a rich stracciatella.

Ingredients
1 pound ground beef
Bread crumbs, moistened with a little water
1 egg, beaten
1 clove garlic, chopped
Fresh flat-leaf parsley, chopped
Pepper
1 cup grated pecorino
Beef stock
1 pound ricotta
5 eggs, beaten

To make the meatballs: combine the ground beef, bread crumbs, egg, garlic, parsley and pepper to taste, and 2 ounces of the pecorino, then form the mixture into small meatballs. Place these in a large saucepan and pour on plenty of boiling stock to immerse completely.

Prepare a mixture of the ricotta, 5 beaten eggs, and the remaining grated pecorino. As soon as the soup comes back to a boil, add this mixture, stirring gently with a fork to form ribbon-like strands as it firms. Add fresh ground black pepper at the last moment.

Variations

The most important variation to note is that in the past meatballs were not included. The mixture remained in a semi-liquid state because of the lack of bread crumbs and contained ground meat, ricotta, eggs, cheese and herbs which were poured into the broth.

The Sicilian name of this dish has its roots in the Latin *juscellum* meaning specifically broth or clear soup and not from the Sicilian word *sciusciari*, to blow. However, since it is referred to in other parts of Sicily as *ciuceddu* or *ciusceddu* it could also derive from ancient Sicilian *ciusca, crusca* in Italian, or husk, or from its diminutive *ciuschitedda,* which means large semolina. This could indicate that in ancient times semolina was probably used to prepare this food instead of bread crumbs.

RICE WITH CHESTNUTS
Risu chê pastigghi

This dish is unique to Sicily, and is typical in the Peloritani Mountains. It is found elsewhere in the areas around Palermo (see variations below). Pastigghi or pastiddi *are dried chestnuts, eaten more as a pastime than for anything else.*

Ingredients
   12 ounces (1 1/2 cups) dried chestnuts, outer skins removed
   A small bunch of young fennel greens (leafy tops only)
   4 tablespoons extra-virgin olive oil
   1/4 cup grated pecorino
   Sea salt
   Rice [3 cups cooked equals 4 servings]

Soak the chestnuts in water to cover overnight. Rinse them next day and boil them for a long time in a small amount of water, then gradually break them up with a fork to form a purée.

Blanch the fennel greens and drain (reserving the liquid) and chop roughly. Add them to a medium skillet coated with olive oil, then over low heat add the chestnut purée, pecorino, salt to taste, and a soup ladle of cooking water from the fennel, mixing well. Add the boiled rice to the mixture, combine and serve warm.

Variations

Some prefer to add enough water to the chestnut and fennel mixture to allow the rice to be cooked together with the other ingredients. In Pollina in particular, and in other areas of the Province of Palermo, pasta is substituted for the rice and fresh chestnuts for the dried version.

SPAGHETTI WITH TUNA
Spaghetti cû tunnu

Recipes for spaghetti with a tuna sauce are common all over the island. This recipe is quite unique and extremely simple to prepare.

Ingredients
- 4 fresh tuna fillets
- Tomato sauce (see page 82)
- Extra-virgin olive oil
- Sea salt
- Fresh flat-leaf parsley, chopped
- 1 pound spaghetti

Slice the fillets into thin strips and fry in a little olive oil in a large skillet until slightly golden on both sides. Drain on paper towels and slice them into slivers. Make a tomato sauce, enough to cover the fillets. Add the fish to the tomato sauce, and cook for another 10 minutes.

Meanwhile, bring a large pot of salted water to a boil and cook the spaghetti until al dente. Drain and transfer to a serving platter.

Add the parsley and dress the spaghetti with the tuna sauce.

coria

LONG-FIN TUNA WITH GARLIC SAUCE
Alalònca cû l'agghiata

This recipe gives me the opportunity to tell you about both the alalònca *(a fish belonging to the tuna family, but different from* tonnetto *and* tombarello *on account of its two long lateral fins) as well as* agghiata. *This garlic sauce, known in antiquity also as grassagghiata, was commonly used either to add strong flavor to otherwise bland foods such as zucchini or eggplant, or to balance the strong "gamey" flavor of foods like tuna, dogfish, sardines, mackerel, beef, etc.*

Ingredients
> Several cloves garlic, finely sliced
> Several tablespoons extra-virgin olive oil
> Sea salt
> White wine vinegar
> Finely chopped mint
> Flour for dusting
> *Alalònca* [or fresh yellow-fin] fillets thickly sliced

Prepare the *agghiata* by frying a large quantity of finely sliced garlic in hot olive oil in a skillet until it turns color slightly, and then covering it with wine vinegar. As soon as the wine vinegar has almost completely evaporated, add salt and chopped mint leaves to taste.

Set out a plate of flour for dusting. Coat the tuna slices in flour and fry them in a large skillet in very hot oil until golden brown on both sides. Immerse the fried fillets into the pan with the garlic sauce. Allow these to rest and serve cold or barely tepid.

STUFFED GRILLED SWORDFISH
Braciulittini di pisci spata

National and regional publications have given us ample descriptions of the unique shape of swordfish, on account of its "sword" that is used to stun small fish when it meets with a shoal of them, and of the way the fish itself is caught with a harpoon.

Ingredients
- Swordfish fillets, thinly sliced
- Soft crustless bread pieces torn up
- 2 cloves garlic, chopped
- Sea salt
- Fresh flat-leaf parsley, chopped
- Extra-virgin olive oil
- Tomato wedges
- Bay leaves

Have your fishmonger cut the swordfish into thin slices. Prepare the stuffing by mixing the bread, garlic, salt, parsley, and enough olive oil to moisten. Place some stuffing on the slices of fish and roll them up, securing each with a toothpick. Thread the rolled fish onto skewers, alternating with tomato wedges and bay leaves. Grill briefly, preferably over hot coals.

Variations

This is a classic recipe in the *cucina povera* tradition, and is also the most authentic because it is not adulterated by other ingredients.

Variations are infinite. The rolled fish, as described above, can be cooked in a preparation like *alla ghiotta* ("for the glutton"), dipped first in red sauce, or in a white sauce, or coated with bread crumbs and then placed in a very hot oven for about 20 minutes.

Variations on the stuffing include the addition of a range of ingredients including pine nuts, raisins, capers, chopped basil leaves, or pecorino.

"Drowned" squid
Calamari affucati

Squid have two small bladders—one with black ink (similar to that found in cuttlefish, and which is discarded in this case) and another with a yellowish liquid that is very much appreciated by gourmets for its hint of musk.

Ingredients
- 1 medium onion, chopped
- 1 clove garlic, chopped
- Medium-sized squid, about 2 pounds, cut into slices, saving contents of yellow bladder
- Glass of dry white wine
- 10 pitted Sicilian green olives, chopped
- 1 tablespoon salted capers, rinsed
- 1 celery heart, chopped, plus smaller leaves
- Fresh flat-leaf parsley, chopped
- 1/2 pound barely ripe tomatoes, peeled, seeded and chopped
- *Peperoncino,* hot red chili pepper, sliced [or dried flakes] to taste

Coat the bottom of a large skillet with olive oil and fry the chopped onion until golden and add the chopped garlic and the squid. Cook for 2 to 3 minutes then add a glass of white wine to the pan and continue cooking for 5 to 8 minutes to allow the wine to evaporate.

Add the pitted olives, capers, chopped celery heart and leaves, parsley, tomatoes, and chili to taste.

It is not necessary to add water at this stage, as the squid will sweat, but a small amount can be added as needed during the time the dish simmers on a very low heat for 1 hour. A few minutes before removing the pan from the heat, add the contents of the yellow bladder, stirring well to combine.

Variation
Some families who prefer a stronger flavor like to add 1 or 2 anchovy fillets at the moment the wine is added.

MUSSEL SOUP
Cozzi a bruoru

Mussels have several other dialect names in Sicily—cozzi, cozza niura, arcella, catacòzzula, anapìnnula—to name a few. The mussels that have been grown for centuries at Ganzirri, an inlet just outside Messina, are much renowned.

Ingredients
    4 1/2 pounds fresh mussels in their shells
    1 medium onion, chopped
    1 clove garlic, chopped
    Extra-virgin olive oil
    1 pound fresh tomatoes, peeled, seeded and chopped
    Fresh flat-leaf parsley, chopped
    1/2 *peperoncino*, hot red chili pepper, sliced [or dried flakes]
    Sea salt
    Fresh basil leaves

Prepare the tomato sauce. In a large pot, fry the chopped onion and garlic in a little olive oil until golden. Add the chopped tomatoes and simmer.

Meanwhile, clean and debeard the mussels, tossing them in a hot pan with a lid until they open. (Discard any that resist opening.)

Remove the mussels from their shells, reserving any liquid. Add the mussels and their cooking liquid to the tomato sauce along with the parsley. Add chili to taste. Adjust the liquid, adding water if necessary, to make a soup. Add salt to taste and serve garnished with a few basil leaves.

new FISH SOUP
Majatica a suppitèdda

Majatica is one of many names indicating the gelatinous mass of newborn fish offspring. Other names are used, varying from province to province and sometimes even from municipality to municipality, which can be very confusing when comparing regional recipes. They include muccu russu, muccbiancu, majatica, nunnatu, jancuneddu, mazzanurara, russelliddu, *and* sfigghiata.

The name majatica, *common in Messina, comes from the dialect word for the month of May* (maju), *this being the month in which fish are more easily caught. This recipe is from San Giorgio.*

Ingredients
    2 pounds *majatica,* newborn fish offspring
    Extra-virgin olive oil
    Sea salt
    Pepper
    18 pitted green olives, chopped
    2 cloves garlic, chopped
    Fresh flat-leaf parsley, chopped

Wash the fish (preferably in seawater). Add this to a saucepan along with half a glass of olive oil, green olives, salt and pepper to taste, and enough water to cover. As soon as the liquid comes to a boil, add the garlic and parsley. Lower the flame and simmer gently for 5 minutes.

Braised Silver Scabbard Fish or Cutlassfish
Mavestu, o spatula, in umitu

This variety of cutlassfish (Lepidopus caudatus), *with its characteristic long shiny silver body in the shape of a ribbon or banner, is common in the Mediterranean and is known by many names:* spatola, pesce bandieri, pesce fiamma. *In Sicily it is called* pisci sciabbula, mavestu, argintinu, *and* u brellande. *Generally, it is sliced and fried or braised in a tomato sauce.*

Ingredients
  1 medium onion, chopped
  Extra-virgin olive oil
  1 pound tomatoes, peeled, seeded and chopped
  Fresh basil leaves, chopped
  1 clove garlic, chopped
  Silver scabbard fish or cutlassfish, sliced
  Flour for dusting
  1/2 glass dry white wine
  Fresh flat-leaf parsley, chopped
  Several young fennel leaves
  1/2 *peperoncino,* hot red chili pepper, sliced [or dried flakes]
  2 bay leaves
  Sea salt

Prepare a sauce. Coat the bottom of a medium skillet with olive oil and add the chopped onion, tomatoes, and basil leaves and simmer.

Set out a plate of flour for dusting. Lightly dust the fish slices in flour.

In a large skillet, heat some olive oil and fry the garlic together with the slices of fish until colored on both sides. Add the white wine and allow this to evaporate. Add the tomato sauce, parsley, fennel leaves, chili, and bay leaves. Add salt to taste and bring to a boil. Lower the heat and simmer gently for 30 minutes.

SWORDFISH PIE
'Mpanata di pisci spata

This is the first 'mpanata we present and being from Messina it naturally features swordfish, a favorite there.

Ingredients
>   Flour for dusting
>   2 pounds swordfish, sliced
>   Extra-virgin olive oil
>   1/2 pound tomatoes, peeled, seeded, and chopped
>   Black olives, roughly chopped
>   1 celery heart, chopped
>   1 tablespoon pine nuts
>   1 tablespoon raisins
>   Sea salt
>   Pepper
>   4 ounces fresh *caciocavallo,* diced
>   Fresh bread dough

Dust the fish with flour and fry the slices in a large skillet after coating the bottom with olive oil.

In a large bowl, mix half a glass of olive oil, the tomatoes, a handful of olives, the celery heart, pine nuts, raisins, salt and pepper to taste, and the *caciocavallo*. Immerse the fried fish in this mixture.

Line the bottom and sides of an ovenproof dish with bread dough and fill with the fish mixture. Cut another sheet of dough to cover the top and seal by folding and pinching the edges together. Bake in a preheated 400° oven for 30 to 40 minutes.

John Dory **Pisci jaddu**

THIS is "Saint Peter's fish" from the well-known biblical story. The name for this species—*pisci jaddu* (rooster fish)—is derived from its splendid color and shape.

Scorpion Fish **Scrofanu**

THIS is the case in other species, like the several varieties of scorpion fish: *scrofanu 'mpiriali*, black scorpion; and *cipudda, gaddarana, capiddazza,* red scorpion.

Some other types are *scrofanu macchiettato, scrofanu tignusu,* and *occiu beddu,* (beautiful eyes); spotted scorpion; and *scrofanu bruno, fascianu,* and *cipudda,* brown scorpion fish.

All these varieties are usually used in soups, but can also be boiled, filleted and accompanied with a sauce.

Messina Stockish **Pisci stoccu**

STOCKFISH, although they belong to the cod family, differ from a similar variety—the *baccalà* or Atlantic cod. Stockfish are caught in Norway and Ireland and are processed differently. Immediately after the catch, the heads and entrails are removed, and they are threaded onto sticks, "stoch-fish" in the local language, hence "stick-fish." They are then left to dry in the fresh air, in the sun and wind, and finally salted. The processed fish looks like wrinkled cardboard, rigid to the touch with an almost wood-like texture, and white flesh that is almost odorless. In dialect it is called *pisci stoccu, piscistuoccu, stoccafissu,* and *stoccu.*

It is particularly prized in Messina, where it was introduced for the first time into Europe during the Norman invasion. There is to this day still a great deal of confusion among consumers, and not only Sicilians, who mistake *pisci stoccu* for *baccalà* and vice-versa.

STOCKFISH MESSINA-STYLE
Pisci stoccu a missinisa

Ingredients
> 2 pounds stockfish, prepared as below and sliced
> 1 onion, chopped
> 2 cloves garlic, minced
> Extra-virgin olive oil
> Dry white wine
> 1 pound tomatoes, peeled, seeded and chopped
> Sea salt
> Pepper
> 1 tablespoon salted capers, rinsed
> Handful of pitted green olives
> 1 carrot, diced
> 1 celery heart, chopped
> 1 tablespoon pine nuts
> 1 tablespoon raisins
> 2 potatoes, peeled and diced

The correct preparation of this fish is very important. First, it must be beaten with a wooden rolling-pin to break up the fibers of the meat. It must then be left to soak for 4 to 6 days in plenty of water, which should be changed regularly as the fish will swell to double its original size and weight. After soaking, the fins, cartilage, tail, and scales must be removed. The skin is usually left on so that the fish will not break up during cooking. The skin also adds to the overall flavor.

Coat the bottom of a large skillet with olive oil and fry the onion and garlic until golden. Add the fish and cook briefly together. Pour in a glass of dry white wine and, once this has evaporated, add the chopped tomatoes, salt and pepper to taste, then simmer for 1 hour. Add the capers, green olives, carrot, celery heart, pine nuts, raisins, and potatoes. Cook until the potatoes are done. The liquid should be quite thick. Add salt and pepper to taste.

Variations

Some prefer to use black olives instead of green.

In two ancient recipes, we find the addition of 3 to 4 winter pears (of the very hard variety known as ’mputiri) as well as potatoes in one, and a handful of sundried zucchini in the other. Both ingredients have gradually disappeared from current use.

STOCKFISH AND "STUFFED BELLIES"
Pisci stoccu e ventri chini a ghiotta

The term a ghiotta *("for the glutton") here, indicates a specific combination of ingredients typical in this dish. For the term* ventri chini, *stuffed bellies, see variations below.*

Ingredients
> Extra-virgin olive oil
> 30 pitted green olives
> 1 celery heart and small, tender leaves, chopped
> Handful of salted capers, rinsed
> 1 1/2 pounds potatoes, peeled and diced
> 1/2 cup tomato sauce (see page 82)
> 3 tablespoons tomato paste
> Prepared stockfish, sliced (see previous recipe)
> Sea salt

Add olive oil to a large stockpot and gently fry the olives, celery, and capers. Coat the bottom of a skillet with olive oil and fry the potatoes on high heat until slightly golden, then add them to the olive mixture along with the tomato sauce and paste. Add enough water to cover and bring to a boil. Once the mixture is boiling, add the stockfish, lower the heat, and simmer for 30 minutes, giving the mixture a frequent gentle stir. When fully cooked, add salt to taste.

Variations

An interesting variation utilizes the belly of the stockfish, called the *ventre*, which is sold separately in the area around Messina. The flesh is rather fatty and therefore more flavorful. The bellies can be added to the standard recipe above for additional flavor, or can be prepared alone—stuffed with a mixture of olives, capers, celery, bread, and cheese—and served in a tomato sauce. This is what gourmets prefer, the *ventri chini, ventri ripiene,* or stuffed belly variation.

Sosizzùni, Ficazzi, Carrubbeddi

THESE are mentioned more as a curiosity than to supply actual recipes as these fish sausages are not prepared in the home. During the cleaning of tuna, certain edible parts of the fish deemed unsuitable for sale are collected, cut into pieces, and with the addition of salt and pepper are preserved like salami. According to their size, they have different names. The largest are called *sosizzùni,* large sausages. Those in a bulbous form like a fig are called *ficazzi,* or large figs. *Carrubbeddi,* little carobs, are the smallest. The production of these sausages has always been a specialty of Milazzo.

Detail of Messina's bell tower

beef rolls messina-style
Braciulini a missinisa

These are small pieces of beefsteak that have been pounded then stuffed. Common in all provinces of Sicily, the ingredients in the stuffing in this version are typical of Messina.

Ingredients
  Beefsteaks, approximately 4-inch squares

  Stuffing
  Bread crumbs
  Extra-virgin olive oil
  Fresh flat-leaf parsley, chopped
  Caciocavallo, sliced
  Fresh basil leaves
  Sea salt
  Pepper
  1 onion, thickly sliced
  Fresh bay leaves

Pound the steaks with a meat tenderizer until thin. Mix the ingredients for the stuffing: bread crumbs, olive oil, parsley, salt and pepper to taste. Place a portion on each piece of meat, together with a slice of *caciocavallo.*

Roll the meat to enclose the stuffing and secure with a toothpick. Thread the beef rolls onto skewers, alternating each with a slice of onion and a bay leaf, and grill.

KID MESSINA-STYLE
Caprettu a missinisa

*This recipe originally specified the meat of a particular breed raised in the Peloritani
Mountains overlooking Messina.*

Ingredients
    2 pounds kid meat
    Lard
    1 onion, sliced thinly
    Fresh rosemary leaves
    Sea salt
    Pepper
    12 ounces (1 3/4 cups) tomatoes, peeled, seeded and chopped

Cube the meat, rinse it, pat dry with paper towels, and smear each piece with a bit of lard.
Place the meat in a large ovenproof dish, cover with the slices of onion, a sprinkling of
rosemary leaves, salt and pepper, and tomatoes. Bake in a preheated 400° oven for 1 hour.

Variation
A handful of pitted, chopped black olives and a sprinkling of dry white wine halfway
through baking can be substituted for tomatoes.

MUTTON MONTALBANESE
Castratu a muntalbanisa

*Montalbano Elicona is a mountain town near Messina noted for its special meat production.
This is a typical recipe of the area.*

Ingredients
    Mutton
    Extra-virgin olive oil
    Sea salt
    Pepper
    Sprigs of fresh rosemary
    Fresh oregano leaves
    1 clove garlic, chopped

Prepare a marinade. Stir together an abundant amount of olive oil, salt and pepper to taste, fresh rosemary, oregano, and garlic. Coat the pieces of mutton well in the marinade and lay the meat in a layer in a baking dish. Halfway through the cooking turn the mutton and baste again in the marinade.

Baking time (1 to 2 hours in a preheated 350° oven) will depend on the oven, and on the age and toughness of the meat.

Variation
Add an onion, sliced thinly, to the marinade.

roast cockerel
Jadduzzu arrustutu

At first glance, this may not seem an original recipe, but the secret lies in the ingredients, and above all, in the method of preparation. It is a specialty of Naso, home of the fabled Grotta di Mercadante.

Ingredients
Small young rooster

For the baste
Freshly-squeezed lemon juice
Extra-virgin olive oil
Sea salt
Pepper
Fresh oregano leaves
Fresh flat-leaf parsley, chopped

Parboil the cockerel for about 20 minutes and drain thoroughly. Split the bird lengthwise and transfer the 2 halves to a hot grill. Meanwhile prepare a baste of lemon juice, olive oil, salt, pepper, and the herbs.

Once the first sides exposed to the heat are hot to the touch, lay them cooked-side down in the prepared baste allowing the hot meat to absorb the basting liquid. Then return the meat to the grill, and grill the other sides. Once these are hot, immerse them in the baste again, allowing them to absorb the liquid, and return the chicken to the grill until cooked through.

The Cave of Mercadante is well hidden in the area of Naso. Legend has it that an immense treasure, which no one has been able to find, is hidden in its heart. The devil, flattering credulous people, causes unusual lights and gigantic ghosts all around them, allows the unsuspecting visitor to fill his pockets with gold coins, but will not allow him to leave the cave until he has put them all back.

QUAIL, OT WILD THTUSH
Quagghi, o turùna 'ntianàti

Since ancient times, the Aeolian Islands, apart for a reputation as producers of excellent capers and lentils, have always been a haven for migratory birds, quail among them. In ancient times, the Bishop of the Islands received a tax on each quail taken by hunters. When the indigent in the community turned to the bishop for assistance and alms, he would reply a tempo di quaglie ("when the quails come" or "if and when I receive the taxes").

This recipe originally specified wild quail, but any medium-sized game bird such as thrush, turtledove, or pigeon, as well as farm-raised quail, are suitable.

Ingredients
    Quail or other game birds
    Clove garlic, crushed, for each bird
    Extra-virgin olive oil
    Several cloves garlic
    Sea salt
    Pepper
    Beef or chicken stock

Clean the birds, reserving their livers. Brush the livers with olive oil, and then place them together with crushed garlic clove in the birds' cavities.

Coat the bottom of a large pot with olive oil, add 2 garlic cloves, salt and pepper, then add the birds and lightly brown them on high heat. Remove the garlic and cover the birds with stock. Continue cooking until the stock has reduced and thickened.

Variations
Finely chopped onion can be substituted for the garlic during browning, and fresh flat-leaf chopped parsley can also be added to the stock.

The word *turùna*, thrush, is derived from the Arabic word *thir*.
In Lombardy it is called *tuon*, a word derived from the same origin.

Suffrittu

This recipe is a specialty not only in the areas around Messina, but along the entire Ionian Sea coast. Sometimes simple, sometimes more elaborate, it is always rich in taste, depending on one's prejudices regarding internal organs, and the selection of cuts used.

Ingredients
    Veal and/or pork offal (heart, kidney, lung, etc.)
    Extra-virgin olive oil
    1 clove garlic, chopped
    Fresh bay leaves
    Sea salt
    1 glass red wine
    1 tablespoon *strattu* (tomato extract) diluted with a little water
    Peperoncino, hot red chili pepper, sliced [or dried flakes] to taste

Coat a skillet with olive oil. Dice the meat into bite-sized pieces, then brown them on all sides in the oil with the garlic, bay leaves and salt to taste. Once the juices have reduced, add red wine and allow to evaporate. Stir through some tomato extract, then add chili to taste and simmer until thoroughly cooked.

Variation

In the area around Catania, this *suffrittu* is made with giblets. The variation of this dish calls for the addition of parsley, basil, rosemary, and black pepper. Red wine is also used, but the tomato extract is omitted and beef stock used in its place.

ARTICHOKE HEARTS WITH EGGS
Cacuocciuli a sciusceddu

We will talk about artichokes elsewhere. It's sufficient here to point out that the term sciusceddu on page 37 is often repeated in the Province of Messina.

Ingredients
　　2 pounds artichokes
　　3 eggs, separated
　　Sea salt
　　Pepper
　　Juice of 1 lemon
　　Fresh flat-leaf parsley, chopped

Remove the tough outer leaves, stems, and choke from the artichokes, leaving only the tender hearts. Boil them in salted water until tender. Drain and cut into wedges.

Beat 3 egg yolks together with salt and pepper to taste, lemon juice, and parsley to taste. Beat the whites separately until stiff.

Place the wedges in a medium pot over low heat and pour in the egg yolk mixture, stirring well to combine thoroughly. Fold in the egg whites, and once the mixture has thickened, serve immediately.

CABBAGE WITH TOMATOES
Cavulu cappuciu cû pumaroru

A wide variety of cabbages are grown in Sicily. This recipe calls specifically for the Cappuccio variety.

Ingredient

1 cabbage, about 2 pounds
Extra-virgin olive oil
1/2 onion, choppped
3 cloves garlic, cut into quarters
3 large ripe tomatoes, peeled, seeded and chopped
Sea salt
Pepper
1/2 glass dry white wine

Remove the tougher outer leaves from the cabbage and slice the entire head into strips. Coat the bottom of a large skillet with olive oil and fry the onion until transparent, then add the cabbage, stirring well. Cook together for several minutes. Add the garlic, tomatoes, salt and pepper to taste, and wine. Bring to a boil.

After 5 minutes add 2 glasses of water. Lower the heat and simmer until cooked through.

Under the classification of Brassica there are three types of cabbage: *Oleracea*, *Napus*, and *Rapa* and numerous varieties. The dialect names (whose list I will spare the reader) add to the confusion so that it is difficult to distinguish one cabbage from another. A Sicilian proverb recommends not to eat cabbage before Saint Michael's Feast Day, September 29—"Whoever eats cabbage before St. Michael, either the husband will die or the wife."

fava Beans with Tomatoes
Favi a ghiotta

This recipe calls for dried fava beans, skin intact but with the "eye" removed.

Ingredients
> 2 pounds dried fava beans, shells removed
> Extra-virgin olive oil
> 1 onion, chopped coarsely
> 2 large ripe tomatoes, peeled, seeded and chopped
> Fresh basil leaves, torn
> Sea salt
> *Peperoncino,* hot red chili pepper, sliced [or dried flakes] to taste

Pinch the fava beans [remove the "eye"] and leave them in water to cover overnight. Boil the soaked beans in salted water until plump and the centers are soft, although not quite cooked through. Remove from the heat and gently drain, retaining a ladle of the water. As soon as they are sufficiently cool to handle, remove and discard the skins.

Coat the bottom of a large skillet with olive oil and fry the onion until golden, add the tomatoes, basil, salt and chili to taste, and then the fava beans. Dilute with the ladle of hot water and simmer for 20 minutes.

EGGPLanT In TomaTo sauce
Milinciani a ficatieddu

There is no other vegetable that lends itself to as many different methods of preparation. Two recipes follow, but a third deserves to be mentioned —milinciani abbuttunati ("buttoned-up" eggplant) that is made in Ucria.

Ingredients
    2 pounds eggplants, peeled and diced
    Extra-virgin olive oil
    3 salted anchovies, deboned
    3 cloves garlic, chopped
    10 ounces (1 1/2 cups) tomatoes, peeled, seeded, and chopped
    Fresh basil leaves
    Fresh mint leaves
    2 tablespoons soft crustless bread, torn in pieces
    Sea salt

Coat the bottom of a a large skillet with olive oil and fry the diced eggplant. In another pan, dissolve the anchovies in a little heated olive oil. Add the garlic, tomatoes, and a few basil leaves. Cook for approximately 10 minutes, then add the eggplant and several mint leaves and bring to a boil. Continue to cook this for 15 minutes.

Sprinkle with bread pieces, salt to taste, and transfer to a serving dish.

Variation
After sprinkling with soft crustless bread pieces, place in a very hot oven to toast the bread topping.

EGGPLANT AND ONION SALAD
'Nsalata di milinciani e cipuddi

Ingredients
>   2 large whole eggplants
>   1 whole onion
>   Extra-virgin olive oil
>   Sea salt
>   Fresh oregano leaves
>   Fresh mint leaves
>   2 cloves garlic, finely chopped
>   Wine vinegar

Boil the two eggplants whole, until cooked through. Peel and slice them and set aside to drain and cool. Boil the onion and slice it when cooked through. Toss the eggplant and onion in a salad bowl with olive oil, salt and pepper to taste, oregano, mint, garlic, and wine vinegar. (The garlic can be cut into halves and later removed, if a milder flavor is desired.) Set aside for a few hours so the flavors combine, tossing frequently.

BAKED POTATOES
Patati 'nfurnati

Despite the bland name, these are quite distinctive.

Ingredients
>   Potatoes, peeled and sliced into discs
>   Mature, fresh tomatoes, peeled, seeded, and chopped
>   Onion, very thinly sliced
>   Cloves garlic, finely chopped
>   Fresh oregano leaves
>   Fresh basil leaves
>   Pepper
>   Sea salt
>   Extra-virgin olive oil

Place potatoes in a large ovenproof dish, together with the tomato, onion, garlic, oregano, basil, and pepper and salt to taste. Sprinkle with olive oil. The quantities used are according to individual taste and the quantity of potatoes. Combine well and bake in a preheated 350° oven for 45 minutes.

BAKED PEPPERS
Pipi 'nfurnati

The ideal way to cook peppers in Messina, or wherever people have access to a charcoal grill, is by slicing and roasting them directly over the coals, and then peeling and dressing them with olive oil, salt and peperoncino. But the following is also an excellent alternative.

Ingredients

Extra-virgin olive oil
2 cloves garlic, finely chopped
Sea salt
Fresh basil leaves, roughly chopped
Fresh flat-leaf parsley, chopped

12 black olives, pitted and roughly chopped
2 to 3 large bell peppers, cut in halves, seeded, then cut into pieces
Bread crumbs
1 tablespoon salted capers, rinsed

Generously coat the bottom of an ovenproof dish with olive oil and stir in the garlic, salt to taste, basil and parsley, followed by the olives and the peppers. Combine well. Sprinkle with bread crumbs and capers. Bake in a preheated 350° oven for 30 minutes.

ROASTED MEADOW MUSHROOMS
Funci picurini arrustuti

Many varieties of mushrooms are grown in Sicily, including the porcini variety. This particular variety, the picurini, *or meadow mushroom, belongs to the genus* agaricus campestris *and is distinguished by a flat semispherical cap with pink gills (covered by a thin white membrane when the mushroom is young) which become chocolate brown as the mushroom matures.*

Ingredients

Extra-virgin olive oil
Sea salt
Pepper

2 cloves garlic, chopped
Fresh flat-leaf parsley, finely chopped
Flat mushrooms

In a large bowl, mix some olive oil, salt, pepper, garlic and parsley, enough to cover mushrooms. Remove the stems from the mushrooms, leaving only the flat caps, wipe them clean with a damp paper towel or soft brush, but do not wash them. Toss them gently in the oil and herb mixture until thoroughly coated. Place on the grill until one side is cooked. Remove and coat with oil and grill the other side.

cheese

Sicily is renowned for several varieties of sheep's milk and cow's milk cheese. The products of San Fratello and San Piero Patti excel, as do the following regional specialty cheeses, each having distinctive characteristics.

Carcagnu

A distinctive type of *caciocavallo* cheese made from a blend of sheep and cow milk, typical of the Messina area and especially of Patti. It is quite sharp even when young.

Majurchinu

A sheep's milk cheese produced predominantly in the region of Messina (Maletto, Novara di Sicilia, and Tripi). It is similar to the *bruntisi* variety produced at Bronte near Catania.

Its Sicilian name is probably derived from Maiorca, in that it is similar to the cheese variety made on that island.

'Ncannistratu

Another cheese made from sheep's milk, whose name is derived from the *canestro* (small wicker basket) in which it is left to mature. Among the most authentic and the best are those from Mistretta and Torregrossa.

It derives from the Latin *canistrum,* a wicker basket for various uses, among which a special one is used to contain and shape cheese. It's interesting to point out that ricotta cheese is still sold in small bamboo containers known as *fiscedda,* from the Latin *fiscella,* another type of small container.

Provole

This has a similar consistency to that of *caciocavallo* and a shape like a wine flask. Those from Capizzi and Sant' Angelo in Brolo are exceptionally good. In the Peloritani Mountains, the same cheese is called *caciocavadduzzi* ("little cacio horses") and is shaped into small horses as if they were toys, and sold with red ribbons round their necks. (The ones made in Floresta are special.)

Ricotta salata e infornata

The salted ricotta of Patti and the baked ricotta of Cesarò are noted for their quality and taste.

onion frittata
Piscirova ccâ cipudda

A simple and rustic little dish, but one with great flavor.

Ingredients
2 large onions, sliced thickly
Extra-virgin olive oil
6 eggs
Sea salt
Pepper
Fresh flat-leaf parsley, chopped

In a large skillet, fry the onions in olive oil until transparent. In a large bowl, beat the eggs well, together with the salt, pepper, and parsley to taste. Once the onion is done, add it to the eggs, reserving the oil.

Then pour the egg and onion mixture back into the pan over high heat. As soon as it begins to set, turn the frittata and cook the other side until both sides are golden.

messina fruits and sweets

fruits

The region around Messina produces a wide variety of fruit. Most excellent are the cherries (Militello, Rosmarino), figs (Barcellona, Militello), lemons (Roccalumera), and apples (Pettineo, San Pier Noceto). Hazelnuts are particularly good from Barcellona, Ficarra, Montalbano Elicona, Roccella Val Demone, San Salvatore di Fitalia, and Ucria, where both hazelnut and walnut orchards are unforgettable.

sweets

As elsewhere in Sicily, Messina produces enchanting sweets in every shape and form. For the record, we cite the following, as well as those for which recipes are provided: *piparelli; ossi di morto** ("dead man's bones"); *bianco mangiare,* a classic of Frazzano; *marmellata di fichidindia* (cactus fruit jam), especially that from Gallodoro; *biscotti sampiroti* (San Piero cookies from San Piero Patti, hence the name); and *tabelle,* typical in Santa Maria di Licodia.

The hazelwood and the walnut are mysterious trees. Moses' rod, which made water gush out of rock, was made of hazelwood. The divining rods of the douser are also made of the same wood. A branch from this tree was the right weapon against poisonous snakes in the middle ages. The fruits, hazelnuts, are exempt from any kind of magic. They are part of the children's game *fossetta,* and have contributed pleasant evenings as people taste them in delicate nougats, *turruni.*

The walnut has an analogous history. It's surely the most discussed tree in the world. Leaving aside a long list of superstitions, myths, and legends linked to it, I will mention only that *nocino,* walnuts, must be gathered on the night of St. Lawrence, August 10, to make a perfect liqueur.

*Typical biscuits shaped like bones, they resemble bones for the whitish color of their surfaces. They were prepared for the dead. Other biscuits completely different in shape, but with the same taste, are made from the same mixture for different feasts.

carnevale fritters
Castagnoli

This is the name around Messina for the traditional castagnole *fritters made during* Carnevale, *the period preceding Lent. They have different names in other provinces:* gnuocculi *(Siracusa);* scocche *(Mazara del Vallo),* zippule, nastri di monaca *("nun's ribbons") and other similar names in western Sicily.*

Ingredients
  Extra-virgin olive oil
  6 cups durum wheat flour [semolina]
  6 eggs, beaten
  1 teaspoon sea salt
  Confectioners' sugar

In a mixing bowl, add flour and form a well. Pour in the eggs together with the salt. Combine, adding enough water gradually to form a soft dough. Knead on a smooth work surface until smooth and pliable, then divide the dough into quarters and roll out into thin sheets. Cut the dough irregularly into long strips.

Bring a generous amount of olive oil to a boil in a large skillet or heavy-bottomed pot. Fry a few pieces at a time in very hot oil until golden. Transfer the strips onto paper towels on a large plate and let the oil drain briefly. On a serving plate, sprinkle the pieces liberally with confectioners' sugar.

Variations
Apart from the number of eggs used, which can vary, the main variation is in the actual shape of the cookies. They can be long and flat like ribbons, or circular, or in spirals.

HONEY COOKIES
Cosi aruci di meli

These are typical of the area of Messina.

Ingredients
>3 cloves, ground
>Nutmeg
>Cinnamon
>Zest of 1 lemon
>2 cups honey
>2 1/2 cups sugar
>1 egg, beaten
>1 cup almonds, ground
>1 ounce brewers' yeast
>3/4 cup candied lemon and orange peel
>*Farina di maiorca* [cake flour]

In a mortar and pestle, grind the cloves to powder and add a pinch of nutmeg and cinnamon to taste, together with the lemon zest.

In a saucepan, bring about 3/4 cup of water with the honey and sugar to a gentle boil until melted. Let cool. When cooled, add the ground spices, egg, almonds, yeast, and candied peel.

Add the flour in a steady stream and mix until a dough has formed. Place the dough on a cold, greased surface and roll out a thick sheet. Cut into small squares and place on a greased baking sheet. Bake in a preheated 400° oven until golden. Once removed from the oven, brush cookies with a lemon glaze.

Rice Fritters
Crispeddi di risu

These fritters are common throughout the island. They have devotional connotations in some parts, being prepared, for example, on the Feast Day of the Patron Saint of Pedara; at Christmas in San Piero Patti; and for the Feast of St. Joseph in Catania. This is the version from Messina.

Ingredients

Extra-virgin olive oil	*Batter*
1 1/2 cups rice	4 eggs
1 quart milk	Flour
1/3 cup sugar	Milk
Vanilla extract	Confectioners' sugar
4 egg yolks	

In a heavy-bottomed pot, bring a generous amount of olive oil to a boil for deep-frying.

In another pot, boil the rice in the milk with the sugar and a few drops of vanilla. After the milk has been absorbed by the rice, remove the pot from heat and allow to cool. When cooled, add 4 egg yolks, and combine thoroughly for a smooth consistency.

Prepare the batter. Stir together 4 eggs with enough flour and milk to form a liquid having the consistency of pancake batter. Form small balls of the rice mixture, coat them in the batter, then deep-fry them until golden. Drain the fritters on paper towels and then dredge each with confectioners' sugar.

Variation

Instead of coating the rice balls in batter, they can be dipped in flour and fried. In this case, they are called *crispeddi a biniddittina* (Benedictine-style fritters) or *crucchetti di risu* (rice croquettes).

Mustazzola di Missina

Messina has two completely different versions of this, both with the same name. Here is one.

Ingredients
1 quart *vinu cottu* (see page 74.)
2 to 3 tablespoons cornstarch
3 ounces (6 tablespoons) walnuts, chopped
3 ounces (6 tablespoons) toasted almonds, chopped
6 cups flour
2 1/2 cups sugar
3/4 cup lard
4 eggs
1 tablespoon *bicarbonato d'ammonio* or *ammonium bicarbonate* [baking soda]
Milk
Candied orange peel (optional)
Cinnamon (optional)
Glaze (optional)

Dissolve the cornstarch in *vinu cottu* in a large pot, stirring in the walnuts and almonds. Bring to a boil, cooking until the liquid has formed a cream, then set aside.

For the pastry, mix the flour, sugar, lard, 4 eggs, baking soda, and enough milk to make a soft, flexible dough. On a smooth work surface, roll this out about 1/8 inch thick and cut into rectangles. Spread a few tablespoons of the walnut cream on the top of each in an S shape. Place on a greased baking sheet and bake in a preheated 350° oven until golden.

Decorate with candied orange peel or cinnamon, or glaze if desired.

calamint pastries
Nipitiddati

The Sicilian name probably derives from nepitella, a variety of mint in the genus Calamintha grandiflora, *a typical Sicilian aromatic herb that at some stage must have figured in this recipe. It is now prepared for the Feast of the Immaculate Conception.*

Ingredients
Dough
6 cups flour
1 3/4 cups sugar
1 cup lard
8 eggs
Sea salt
Milk

Filling
2 eggs
1 1/2 pounds (3 cups) dried figs
8 ounces (1 cup) chopped walnuts
8 ounces (1 cup) chopped, toasted almonds
8 ounces (1 cup) chopped pistachios
7 tablespoons grated chocolate
Cucuzzata: 5 cloves, 1 tablespoon ground cinnamon, and chopped dried orange peel

Prepare the dough with the flour, sugar, lard, eggs, a pinch of salt and enough milk to form a smooth, elastic dough. On a smooth work surface, divide and roll out the well-kneaded dough into thin sheets. Cut out 4-inch circles.

Prepare the filling. Mix together the eggs, dried figs, walnuts, almonds, pistachios, and chocolate. Grind the *cucuzzata* ingredients in a mortar and pestle and add this to the filling mixture, combining thoroughly.

Spoon some of the filling onto each pastry circle and fold each over and press down the edges. With the tip of a sharp knife make two cuts in the shape of an X on each top so that during baking the dough will split open to reveal the filling. Bake in a preheated 350° oven on a greased baking sheet until golden.

Variation
Amounts of filling can be changed, as well as the size of the pastry.

walnut pastries
Nucatuli

This recipe seems to have originated in the Convent of St. Elizabeth in Palermo, and was typically served during Christmas celebrations. The recipe then spread throughout Sicily, taking different names, among which are bifuliddi, nocatole, nucatole, nucatuli, *and even* mucatuli *in the area of Ragusa. This recipe is from the Province of Messsina.*

Ingredients
> 6 cups flour
> 3/4 cup lard
> 1 cup sugar
> 2 egg yolks
> 1 glass rose water, or other flower-based waters, or vanilla extract
> Sweet white wine

> *For the filling*
> 2 cups blanched almonds
> 1 3/4 cups honey
> Ground cinnamon
> 1 or 2 tablespoons of rose water

In a large bowl, combine the flour, lard, sugar, egg yolks, rose water, and enough wine to make a dough. On a smooth work surface, roll out into thin sheets and cut out small circles.

Prepare the filling. In a large pot, combine the almonds, honey, cinnamon, and a few spoons of rose water. Stir to combine over low heat to produce a filling having the consistency of a tomato sauce. Spread the filling on half the pastry circles, covering each with the other circles. Seal the outer edges of pastry by pressing together with the tines of a fork. Bake in a preheated 350° oven on a greased baking sheet until golden.

Variations

There are many variations throughout Sicily, both in the ingredients in the filling and the dough or the shape of the pastries. Only the name is the same.

Originally the name was incorrectly assumed to derive from the Arabic *naqal* (dried fruit), but it is most likely derived from the late Latin word *nucatus,* or walnut, which were the original nuts used in this recipe—and which have now been replaced by almonds.

ALMOND RINGS
Ciambelli di mennuli

Typical are those from Castroreale Terme.

Ingredients
> 6 cups flour
> 5 cups sugar
> Zest of 1 orange
> 1 tablespoon *bicarbonato d'ammonio* or *ammonium bicarbonate* [baking soda]
> Almond milk or water
> 2 cups almonds, peeled and chopped

In a large bowl, mix together the flour, sugar, orange zest, and baking soda, adding enough almond milk or water to form a dough. Knead the dough on a smooth work surface, adding the chopped almonds. Roll out a sheet a bit less than 1 inch thick and cut out small doughnut shapes. Place these on a greased baking sheet and bake in a preheated 350° oven until golden.

BLACK RICE
Risu niuru

In the area around Messina, this dish is prepared to perfection at Castroreale Terme. It has been a traditional sweet and is made especially for the Feast of the Black Madonna of Tindari and for Christmas.

Ingredients
> 4 cups rice
> 2 quarts milk
> Sugar
>
> 2/3 cup dark chocolate
> Confectioners' sugar
> Cinnamon

In a heavy-bottomed pot, boil the rice in the milk, adding more milk until the rice is cooked. Remove from heat. Melt the chocolate in a double-boiler together with sugar to taste. Blend the chocolate and sugar sauce into the rice mixture. Dust each serving with confectioners' sugar and cinnamon.

Variations

These include changes in the quantities, the addition of crushed toasted almonds and diced candied fruit, or using grated chocolate as a dusting rather than the sauce.

Pinecones *Pignulata*

IF you are asked what is the special dessert of Messina, you can't go wrong saying *pignulata*, which is enjoyed traditionally at Christmas and Easter, but now prepared all year. Some claim it originated in Borgetto in the Palermo area, but they are probably confusing it with the *pignuccata*, which although similar to it, is something else that is made all over in Sicily. (For the recipe, see *pignuccata* in the Ragusa section).

It appears particularly during *Carnevale* at Partinico, Furci Siculo, Buscemi, and elsewhere. Both names, *pignulata* and *pignuccata*, suggest *pinoli* (pine nuts, which are entirely absent from both) but actually derive from the look of the finished form of the assembled sweet, which is similar to a pinecone. Small pastry balls are mounded together and bound by either a lemon or chocolate glaze, so that they look like pinecones that have been split in half. One of the secret ingredients in the dough is some form of alcohol added to the flour and eggs to help the dough rise. The lemon glaze, *marangola*, combines egg whites, sugar and lemon juice.

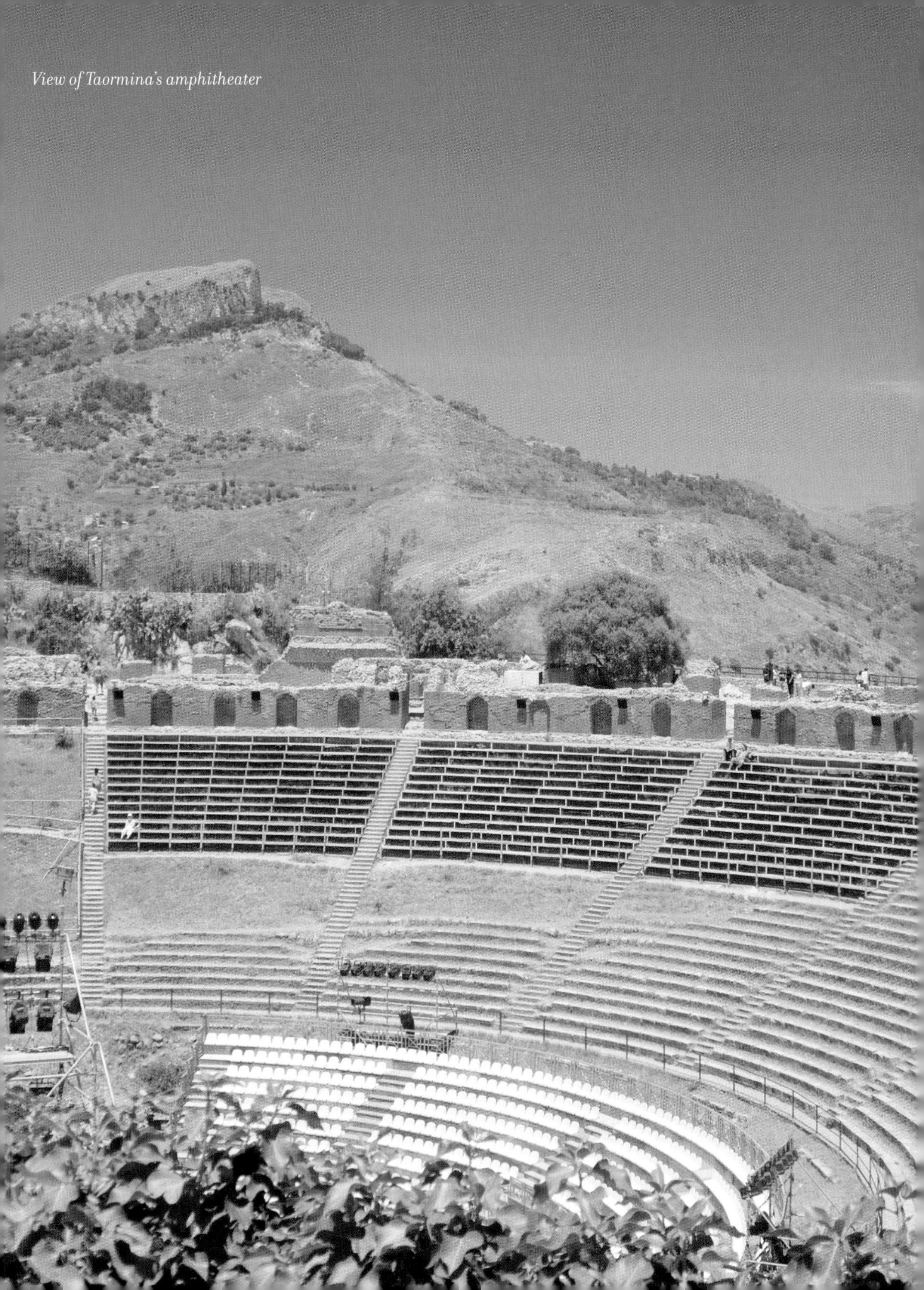
View of Taormina's amphitheater

LITTLE WEDGES
Spicchiteddi

Ingredients
- 6 cups flour
- 3 1/2 cups lard
- Cinnamon
- *Vinu cottu*
- Blanched whole almonds
- Honey

Combine the flour, lard, cinnamon to taste, and as much *vinu cottu* as is required to produce a smooth, pliable dough. On a smooth work surface, roll out the dough into several thick sausages, and then slice these into disks, which in turn are quartered so they look like orange wedges. Press an almond into the top of each wedge and bake in a preheated 400° oven until golden. Once baked, brush with melted honey or *vinu cottu*.

Pottery in Taormina

Vinu cottu Cooked wine

Here is the traditional method. It's nothing other than the Latin *Sapa* and it is still made in the same way among various families. You start with the fresh pressing of wine grapes [grape must], adding orange rinds and lemon leaves, which is boiled on a slow, simmering fire until its volume is reduced by two-thirds from the initial quantity. Out of nine liters of must you will obtain only three liters of cooked wine. To make a clear product you will need to let the liquid cool and rest for about two days. Then you throw out the sediments and filter the wine. Cooked wine prepared in this manner can be kept for many years, but it's better to prepare it yearly. You can use it in special desserts.

WINES

THERE are two *Denominazione di Origine Controllata (DOC)* wines, or Wines of Designated Origin, in the area of Messina. One, *Faro*, a dry red wine of ruby color, has an alcoholic content between eleven and one-half and thirteen percent, and is produced in the Messina area. The other, *Malvasia di Lipari,* a soft white Muscat-style wine with an eleven and one-half percent alcohol content—and up to twenty percent in the case of the dessert wine of the same name—is produced in the archipelago of the Aeolian Islands, in particular on Salina and Stromboli.

The Italian government has identified and awarded the DOC to unique and significant wines in specific regions or towns. Their geographical origin determines quality and particular characteristics.

Among the most renowned table wines are the following labels: *Capobianco, Caporosé, Caporosso, Eolo* (whites, reds, and rosé), *Isolano* (red), *Mamertino* (white, red, and rosé), *Nettuno* (white, red, and rosé), *Salina* (white, red, and rosé), and *Suaviter* (white, red, and rosé). Renowned dessert wines are *Moscato Liquoroso* and *Zibibbo Liquoroso*.

LIQUEURS

Latti di vecchia (Old Woman's Milk Liqueur)

One of the oldest homemade fortified liqueurs, it is also found in provinces outside Messina and in some southern regions.

Ingredients
    1 quart goat or other milk, freshly milked
    5 cups sugar
    1 quart unflavored [pure, distilled] 90-proof alcohol
    Zest of 1 orange or lemon, or vanilla

On low heat, dissolve the sugar in the milk. As soon as the liquid has cooled, add the alcohol and a pinch of orange or lemon zest. Transfer to a large flask then cork and shake the contents together. Let rest for 14 days, taking care to shake the flask at least twice a day. After that period, strain and bottle.

Taormina

catania, because of its dynamic and cosmopolitan nature, has lost so many of its gastronomic traditions that identifying authentic specialities requires a magnifying glass. Nevertheless it boasts a table that is lively, colorful, and full of imagination and good cheer—like its people who live, after all, in the place inhabited by the equally imaginative magician Eliodorus[1] and the gastronome Emir Mohammed ibn Timma (or Thumma)[2] who invented the chicken pie.

Refined in their tastes, the Catanese love strong and distinctive flavors, as long as they are harmonious, and they love elaborate dishes as long as they are balanced in the final result.

In most cases, first courses are not unlike those prepared on the rest of the island. Where they differ, the variations are due to the creativity and exuberance of local cooks. I refer to the *risu niuru di sicci (ripiddu nivicatu),* squid ink risotto, dedicated to Mount Etna, to *pasta a la Norma,* and to several other *cucina povera* recipes that surprise with the goodness and balance of their ingredients. Regarding the latter, I refer to the pasta *rinfusa,* dressed with a sauce made from sliced salted anchovies with bread crumbs in olive oil; and the classic *maccarruna di setti purtusi* ("macaroni of the seven holes"),[3] ingeniously made pasta traditionally prepared for *Carnevale* that emerges from a press with seven holes and is dressed with a pork-based *ragù.*

The fish market at Catania, open every day of the year, offers an unforgettable array of fish and seafood. Here, presentation counts for much—the larger fish have their heads and tails strung together to give the body a curvature that makes them almost look alive. There is also a wide price range offered. (In 1995 it was still possible to purchase about two pounds of sardines and other small species for about one dollar while larger and less common fish cost slightly more.) This market is largely supplied by the small fleet that plies the coastal waters. Small boats in private hands with an eye and the names of saints painted on either side of the prow[4] grant the fishermen a miraculous catch.

Several dishes are worthwhile recalling for their exceptional creativity. The *alici all'arancia,* anchovies with orange, prepared with orange segments, green olives, pine nuts, white wine, and black pepper; and *masculinu,* a variety of anchovy having a characteristic

1. Heliodorus, known also as Liodorus or Theodorus, was a great and powerful magician, second only to Simon the magician. Giulio Filoteo Omodei in his *Sommario degli uomini illusri di Sicilia* (a manuscript in the Municipal Library of Palermo) related that this man was capable of transforming himself and others into any type of animal. He also had the gift of ubiquity. He rode an elephant, which is the symbol of the city, but he was disliked by the Catanese for other motives as well. For this reason they turned to the Emperor of the Eastern Roman Empire to get rid of him. The Emperor sent Captain Heraclitus to arrest him and the two went back to Constantinople. But Heliodorus suddenly disappeared and reappeared in Catania. The good Heraclitus made the sea journey between Constantinople and Catania twice but both times his prisoner disappeared and flew back to his native Catania. The last time that Heraclitus was in Constantinople with his prisoner, his wife, who was furious because of the forced absence of her husband, hurled all kinds of insults against him and finally spit in his face. Heliodorus made her regret her action devising the greatest magic of all time to bring ridicule on the woman. He extinguished all fires in the city. The only fire avilable in the whole city came out of the woman's behind. Thus the poor woman was forced to expose her buttocks to the citizens of the city who went to her as the only source of fire.

2. Michele Amari (both in his *History of the Muslim in Sicily* and in the *Biblioteca Arabo-Sicula*) gave us his exact name as Ibn at Timmha (or Thummah) Muhammad ibn Ibràhim. He said that he was certainly not born a plebeian and he became the lord of Siracusa and then of Catania, (1019). However, he said nothing about the chicken pie he was supposed to have invented. I don't know where Felice Cunsolo found the recipe he recorded in his *Guida gastronomica d'Italia (Gastronomic Guide to Italy)*, ed. by the Istituto Geografico De Agostini, 1975) that I will summarize for the interested reader. Take a round bread and remove its soft part; stuff it with chicken fillets previously cooked and add chopped toasted almonds, pistachios, capers, parsley, and beaten eggs. Seal the round bread and moisten it with broth and then bake it in the oven.

3. A type of tubular pasta that had, as the name says, seven holes internally. The pasta makers used a special mold for this purpose. It were favored over other types because the sauce could dress them more easily and became richer in flavor because the ground meat in the *ragù* sauce could enter the cavities.

4. The sailors of the Mediterranean painted an eye on the prow of their boats or ships as a symbol of their vigilance against the dangers of the sea. The sailors of the Catania area kept this tradition and indeed strengthened it. In baptizing their boats with the names of saints or the Madonna, they added a sacred aspect to the profane symbolism.

5. Two types of algae are utilized by a few admirers in the Catania area: the *curaddina,* eaten raw as any salad; and one called *mauru* that generally is fried in a pan.

6. The lake of Lentini that today is called Biviere, on the border between the Provinces of Siracusa and Catania, was created, according to the myth, by Hercules. It was always rich in fish and especially eels.

7. Frogs have a rich history in myth, religion and legend, generating a number of superstitions. From Heket, the Egyptian goddess with the human body and the head of a frog, we go to the Greek and Roman Batracomancy, a form of divining that interpreted the croaking of frogs. The populace of Sicily have always believed that the souls of the dead reside in frogs to expiate their sins. (Anyone who kills a frog "will suffer seven years of bad luck.") Naturally the inhabitants of Palermo have always disregarded the notion.

torpedo shape and shiny skin that is prepared in hundreds of different ways—including deep-frying in oil, accompanied only by garlic and parsley and, contrary to every culinary rule, paired with the sharp taste of *pecorino,* a sheep's milk cheese. Another regional specialty is *sangunusu abbuttunatu,* a small variety of tuna, stuffed. And finally, in Catania, and nowhere else in Sicily, a variety of seaweed is sold that many people enjoy raw in salads.[5]

As for freshwater fish, we must not forget eels, not only those from the Biviere di Lentini [a lake], but also those caught in the Simeto River by fishermen who sell them to motorists stopped at the traffic light right on the bridge. This is on the road from Catania to Siracusa.[6]

In the surrounding foothills of Mount Etna, certain meat dishes are worthy of note: *caprettu chinu,* tender stuffed kid; and *jadduzzu arrustutu,* roast cockerel, the traditional dish of the area as well as of Palagonia and its adjacent municipalities for the Feast Day of Saints Cosimo and Damian. And the list goes on—*trippa fritta,* fried tripe, *zinènu abbuttunatu,* stuffed intestines, and so on.

The citizens of Paternò and their neighbors share the unique privilege of being the only consumers of frogs in Sicily. In ancient times, this entire area was a swamp, the natural habitat of frogs. As is the case with any rich natural resource, this is taken advantage of to the maximum.[7]

The area around Catania is dedicated to the cultivation of fruits of every type, especially the *tarocchi* orange variety, famous all over the country. The slopes of Mount Etna support vigorous vineyards, a miracle of nature considering that the vines grow and sustain themselves on volcanic soil.

catania FIRST courses

pasta WITH SICILIAN TOMATO sauce
Pasta ccâ sarsa

Tomato sauce, called simply sarsa, *"sauce," is the simplest of preparations and features more often than any other component in Sicilian cooking—especially in summertime —but not everyone prepares it in the same way.*

If you give two pounds of the same type of tomato to one hundred Sicilian cooks, you will end up with one hundred different sauces, as there are as many variables and combinations. Some will start out by frying a selection of ingredients first, others start out with everything cold. Some strain the tomatoes (passed through a fine sieve to remove the seeds and skin), others chop the seeded flesh roughly, and still others use the entire

fruit—skin, seeds and all. The recipe can include or exclude, in part or completely, a variety of other ingredients such as onions, garlic, red hot pepper, and basil. Some will swear to the use of a pinch of bicarbonate of soda to cut acidity or sugar to add sweetness. Cooking times also vary, from a few minutes to much longer, which results in either a very liquid sauce, a thicker, creamier consistency, or a very dense, dry sauce.

I could say that the pasta, boiled and drained, are dressed with the sauce (one of the many) and that could be the end of it. But it is worthwhile to offer some of the little techniques, "the little secrets," Sicilian women use to make this dish more pleasing. First of all, a light sprinkling of cheese over the pasta should *precede* the addition of the sauce. Sauce should not be too thick because upon contact with the pasta it would be completely absorbed. The aroma of basil (the smaller, curly-edged variety is ideal) is essential and is added at the last minute, torn fresh over the hot pasta. The addition of fried slices of eggplant, laid on top of the dressed pasta, will improve the whole presentation.

SUNDRIED TOMATOES AND TOMATO EXTRACT
Ciappi, Capuliatu e Strattu

The vast abundance of tomatoes, the "fruit of the sun," has allowed Sicilians not only to eat them fresh, but to preserve them in the following three ways.

Ciappi

Semi-sundried tomatoes, by now well-known in the north of Italy as well, are nothing more than tomatoes that have been cut in half, salted, and allowed to dry in the sun. It is important in this case that they not dry out completely. They are then preserved in jars with olive oil and are famously good as an antipasto as well as an accompaniment for other foods.

Capuliatu

These sun-dried tomatoes take their name from the fact that they need to be cut with the mezzaluna knife and are a variation on *ciappi*. These are completely dried out and usually skinless. They are chopped and also preserved in jars with basil and garlic, and the resulting preparation is used by the spoonful to add flavor to soups or to brighten up a plain omelette, to enrich a vegetable dish, or just for the sheer pleasure of spreading it on a piece of plain or toasted bread.

Strattu

The tomato extract, also called *astrattu* in Palermo, is made in this way: tomatoes are peeled and seeded, then the pulp is briefly boiled with a little salt, sieved and spread over a flat surface to dry exposed to the sun. Each day, this is stirred carefully as the moisture evaporates, and exposed in containers of ever-diminishing size until the correct density is achieved. The expert eye will know the correct moment to preserve this pure "extract of the sun" as it is called. In fact, from 40 pounds of tomatoes one will obtain only 2 pounds of *strattu*, having the consistency of clay. Once it is at this stage, it is rolled into small balls that are polished with a little olive oil and stored with a few basil leaves in jars. And what will it be used for? In Sicily, there is not a sauce or a *ragù* that does not include the use of *strattu*. It is used most predominantly in sauces—especially on the most "important" occasions, dishes for feast days and holidays. It will add a dash of color to even the palest and most insipid broth. In this volume, every time I mention *strattu* in a recipe, the reader should know immediately that I am referring only to this. While there are other industrially made extracts or concentrated pastes, they have little in common with our *strattu*.

The tomato traveled from Perù, its land of origin, to Mexico where Pizarro's sailors found it circa 1530. When it was first imported into Spain and Italy, it was not well received as it was considered toxic. Although grown in southern Italy and in Sicily during the first years of the 17th century, it made its debut on the tables of nobility only in the 1850s.

pasta a la norma

Most people actually call this dish Pasta ccâ Norma. *This is incorrect because* ccâ *in dialect means "with", making Norma a simple ingredient, analogous to* pasta ccâ cucuzza, *pasta with squash. Norma was the main character of the opera by the same name composed by Bellini, to whom the dish was dedicated.* Pasta a la Norma *(Pasta Norma-style) refers specifically to this dish dedicated to Bellini who was from Catania. The authenticity of this classic dish depends on the quality and abundance of the sauce, and above all, on the inclusion—and this is a non-optional essential—of salted ricotta as a condiment.*

Ingredients
> Tomato sauce
> Extra-virgin olive oil
> 2 pounds eggplant, peeled and sliced thinly
> 1 pound spaghetti
> 6 ounces (3/4 cup) *ricotta salata*, grated
> Fresh basil leaves, torn by hand
> *Peperoncino,* hot red chili pepper, sliced [or dried flakes]
> Sea salt

Prepare a simple tomato sauce. In a large skillet, fry the eggplant slices in olive oil and drain them between paper towels, using a weight for maximum drainage. Bring a large pot of salted water to a boil and cook the spaghetti al dente, drain, and transfer to a large bowl. Dress the spaghetti with plenty of sauce and toss with the salted ricotta, torn basil leaves, and chili to taste. Serve on individual plates and garnish with the fried eggplant slices, more sauce, a grating of ricotta, and more basil leaves.

Variation

In the area around Siracusa and at Carlentini in particular, the name *"pasta a la Norma"* is applied to a different dish. Macaroni (not spaghetti) is dressed with a meat and tomato *ragù* (including 10 ounces of ground veal and 6 ounces of ground pork), and baked in a casserole with alternating layers of tomato sauce, fried eggplant, sliced hard-boiled eggs, and cheese.

Ricotta salata has been salted and cured or dried, and is used for grating.

PASTA WITH CHICKPEAS
Pasta chî ciciri

*Pasta with chickpeas is traditionally served in the Catania area
(and also around Agrigento) for the Feast of Saint Joseph. Chickpeas
compete with fava beans as traditional foods served on All Souls'
Day. Chickpeas were among the foods of the very poor. In fact, to
indicate something of little substance or something bland, the saying
was* brodu di ciciri—*chickpea broth. Even today, it is one of the
least expensive beans. Yet I know of several well-to-do people who are
willing to leave their comfortable homes in the dead of winter, to go to
a trattoria, where they serve only legumes, paying dearly for them.*

Ingredients
- 4 cups chickpeas
- 1 large onion, sliced
- Fresh flat-leaf parsley, chopped
- Sea salt
- Thin lasagne sheets
- Extra-virgin olive oil

Soak the chickpeas in water overnight and drain and rinse them out
the next day. Place the chickpeas in a heavy-bottomed casserole (a
terracotta pot with a cover is ideal), with onion slices, parsley, and
salt. Cover completely with cold water, cover the pot, and bring to
a boil. Lower the heat and cook gently for at least 3 hours. Drain,
retaining the cooking liquid. Cook the lasagne sheets in this liquid
until al dente. (The thin sheets of lasagne used traditionally in this
recipe are called *sfilateddi,* referring to the thinness to which the
sheets are rolled out.) Gently remove the cooked sheets. In a large
serving dish, assemble the lasagne sheets between layers of the
chickpea mixture and drizzle with olive oil.

Variations

Some add various other ingredients to the chickpeas as they cook—a
chopped ripe tomato, garlic cloves, fresh rosemary sprigs or
marjoram leaves, and, even better, *peperoncino.*

Mixing a purèe of chickpeas
with onions and honey, Arabs
obtained an aphrodisiac.
We don't know whether it is
a coincidence, but in Sicily
chickpeas are cooked with
onions, a specialty of Gela
to be eaten on December 13,
the day dedicated to St. Lucy.
This requires simply boiling
chickpeas and then dressing
them with honey. The use and
consumption of chickpeas in
Sicily is still very much alive:
you can see it in the *calia,* of
clear Arabic origin, which
identifies boiled chickpeas
and toast to eat as a pastime.
Panelle, thin strips made
from chickpeas flour, can be
eaten fried or sandwiched
in bread (the classic bread
and *panelle* of Palermo) and
as liquid *pulénta* (polenta),
with lard and sausages as is
the tradition in Cesarò in the
Province of Messina.

Many Sicilian writers assure
us that chickpeas played a role
in the history of the island.
During the revolution of 1282
against the Angevins, known
as the Sicilian Vespers, it was
not always possible to identify
the oppressors who hid in the
crowd dressed as civilians.
Thus the revolutionaries
invited the suspects to repeat
the Sicilian word *ciciri,*
chickpeas, (pronounced
chèecheereeh), that the
French could pronounce only
as *Kèekeereeh* or *sèeseereeh.*
Thus *ciciri,* if pronounced
incorrrectly, meant a death
sentence for many.

Pasta with Anchovies
Pasta ccû masculinu

The masculinu *is a variety of anchovy, which is typically torpedo-shaped and silver in color. It's the most beloved blue fish of the Catanese, who appreciate its pleasing though not overpowering taste and its versatility in a variety of recipes.*

Ingredients

    Extra-virgin olive oil
    1 small onion, finely sliced
    2 pounds *masculinu* or other anchovies
    2 cloves garlic, cut into halves
    1/2 pound tomatoes, peeled, seeded and chopped
    Fresh flat-leaf parsley, chopped
    Sea salt
    1 pound spaghetti

Ideally, the fish should be bought freshly caught, with the head removed, and it should be gutted and descaled under running water. In a large skillet or pot, gently fry the onion in olive oil until barely golden. Add the fish, garlic, and tomatoes, with parsley and salt to taste. Bring this to a boil. As soon as it begins boiling, remove the fish bones with a fork (the flesh should separate quite easily). Lower the heat and simmer for about 20 minutes.

Meanwhile, bring a large pot of salted water to a boil and cook the spaghetti al dente, and drain. The sauce should be quite thick, and is used to dress the spaghetti.

PASTA WITH SQUID INK AND RISOTTO WITH SQUID INK

Pasta ccû niuru dî sicci e rìpiddu nivicatu

This dish features the black "ink" taken from squid. There is no doubt that the ink is what gives this dish its distinctive flavor. A comparison between sauces prepared with and without the contents of the ink sac will reveal all.

Ingredients
> 1/4 medium onion, grated
> 2 cloves garlic, chopped
> Extra-virgin olive oil
> 2 pounds squid, cleaned and cut into large and small pieces
> Fresh flat-leaf parsley, chopped
> Pepper
> Tomato paste
> 1/2 pound tomatoes, peeled, seeded, and chopped
> Sea salt
> Ink sacs removed from the squid
> 1 pound spaghetti

Coat the bottom of a large skillet or pot and gently fry a piece of grated onion and garlic. Add the pieces of squid, add parsley, and pepper to taste. After a few minutes add the tomato paste and tomatoes. Salt to taste. (Do not add water, as the squid will release liquid.) After coming to a boil, continue cooking for 25 minutes and only at this final stage add the contents of the ink sacs. Taste for seasoning, stir the ink through, and remove from the heat. Remove the large pieces of squid.

Meanwhile, bring a large pot of salted water to a boil and cook the spaghetti al dente, drain, and transfer to a large serving bowl. Dress the spaghetti with the sauce and top with the large pieces of squid. Serve as a *secondo*, second course.

Rìpiddu nivicatu

Snow-capped risotto, a specialty of Catania, is prepared in a similar fashion. This is rice cooked in the same sauce, then shaped into a cone, topped with a spoonful of ricotta and a dash of tomato sauce. The symbolism is clear. The dish represents Mount Etna—the black rice its lava stones, the ricotta its snowy cap, and the tomato its fiery lava erupting.

raw anchovies
Anciova cruri

In Catania, this dish is also referred to as masculinu. *It has always been a second course (sometimes a combination of first and second), but today it is offered as an antipasto in restaurants. Its name is derived from the Greek word* apya, *meaning small fish, later from the Latin* apua *which became the ancient Italian word* api-usa, *since then becoming the current* acciuga.

Ingredients
- Lemon juice
- Sea salt
- Whole cleaned anchovies, heads cut off
- Extra-virgin olive oil
- Pepper
- Sea salt
- *Peperoncino,* hot red chili pepper, sliced [or dried flakes]
- Fresh flat-leaf parsley, chopped
- 1 clove garlic, chopped

In a large bowl, make a marinade of lemon juice and salt to taste, enough to cover the anchovies. Immerse the anchovies in it and cure for at least 12 hours until the fish become white and tender. Drain them on paper towels and dress with olive oil, pepper and salt. Add chopped chili, parsley, and garlic to taste.

ROASTED GARFISH
Augghi arrustuti

Garfish are well-known due to their long, pointed snout; the dialect name augghi *means "needles." Characteristic also is the tendency for their cooked bones to turn bright emerald green. They are much appreciated in the region of Catania, although a larger variety, called* giganti, *or giants, are caught around Messina.*

Ingredients
> Garfish
> Extra-virgin olive oil
> Sea salt
> Charbroiled tomatoes, dressed *optional*

After cleaning them, roll the garfish into doughnut shapes by inserting the pointed snouts into the body and securing with skewers. Oil them and place on a charcoal grill (or in the oven). Quickly grill over high heat and cook on all sides. Sprinkle with salt and serve piping hot. It is common to serve the fish with whole charbroiled tomatoes, crushed and dressed with oil, salt, minced garlic, parsley, and fresh mint or oregano.

ROASTED STOCKFISH
Pisci stoccu arrustutu

The stockfish that we saw as one of Messina's specialties, which is typical of Riposto as well, has recently become more popular again in this city.

Ingredients
> Stockfish, soaked overnight and rinsed
> Extra-virgin olive oil
> Sea salt
> Pepper
> Juice of 1 lemon

Briefly boil the fish. Drain thoroughly and slice, coating each slice with olive oil, and salt and pepper to taste. Place on a charcoal grill and roast both sides. Serve hot, drizzled with oil and lemon juice.

This is not surprising considering that a small colony of survivors of a plague fled from Messina and settled in Riposto. Their numbers increased after the earthquake of 1692, when others came, bringing along their customs and traditions.

sand lance, catanese-style
Cicireddu a catanisa

The variety of names cicireddu, ciciredda, cicirieddu, *and* cicirello *referring to this fish indicate two entirely different species.* This recipe is for the Sand Lance, measuring up to 6 or 7 inches in the adult, which plays an important role in the fishing industry in Sicily due to its abundance. A pearly-skinned fish with a pleasant taste, it is usually prepared fried.*

Ingredients

2 pounds Sand Lance
1/2 pound fresh tomato, peeled, seeded, and chopped
Extra-virgin olive oil, a glassful
1 tablespoon red wine
Basil and mint leaves torn
2 cloves garlic, chopped
2 tablespoons bread crumbs
4 ounces (1/2 cup) fresh *caciocavallo*, grated
Sea salt
Pepper

Wash and drain the fish, placing them in a baking dish together with the tomato, olive oil, red wine, parsley, torn basil and mint leaves, garlic, bread crumbs, cheese, and salt and pepper to taste. Stir to combine thoroughly, cover with a lid or foil and bake in a preheated 400° oven for 30 minutes.

*The second species, also referred to as *cicireddu* or small eels, are indeed the tiny eels that resemble the Sand Eel except being true eels, these do not have tail fins. The latter species is quite rare and is much sought-after as a delicacy.

BUTTONED-DOWN "BULLET" TUNA
Sangunusu abbuttunatu

Sangunusu refers to a variety of tuna that differs from the others in that it has dark red flesh. Abbuttunatu (buttoned) refers to a typical technique used in Sicily where the stuffing is secured to prevent it from escaping during cooking. Abbuttunatu is found in reference not only to larger fish, but also to poultry and small animals cooked whole. This recipe appears to have originated in the region around Paternò.

Ingredients
>   Medium-sized *sangunusu* "bullet" tuna
>   Extra-virgin olive oil
>   Sea salt
>   *Caciocavallo*, diced
>   1 clove garlic, finely chopped
>   Fresh flat-leaf parsley, chopped
>   Lard
>   Wine vinegar
>   Pepper

Gut and rinse the fish, drying thoroughly with paper towels. Oil the fish inside and out and sprinkle with a little salt. Stuff the cavity with a mixture of *caciocavallo*, garlic, and parsley. Close the cavity by securing it with kitchen twine. Make a series of small incisions in the flank of the fish and insert a small sliver of lard in each cut. Lay the fish in a well-greased baking dish. Whisk together some olive oil, wine vinegar, and salt and pepper to taste, then drizzle over the upper surface.

Bake in a preheated 400° oven for 20 minutes. Remove from the oven and turn the fish over. Drizzle again with whisked olive oil and wine vinegar, and bake for another 20 minutes until cooked through.

STUFFED KID
Caprettu chinu

This stuffed kid is one of the most classic examples of Sicilian Baroque cuisine, which expected and demanded that stuffing provide sumptuous specialties to satisfy both tastes and aesthetics. This is a traditional Easter dish in the foothills of Mount Etna (in particular at Randazzo and Castiglione di Sicilia), where ample ovens exist capable of containing a whole kid. Most homes had ovens in which they baked bread beforehand and they were quite large.

Ingredients

Beef offal (liver, heart, etc), diced
Extra-virgin olive oil
1 onion, finely chopped
Sea salt
Pepper
Fresh flat-leaf parsley, chopped
2 pounds vermicelli

6 ounces (3/4 cup) pecorino, diced
6 ounces (3/4 cup) *caciocavallo*, diced
10 ounces prosciutto, finely sliced in strips
4 to 8 hard-boiled eggs, peeled and chopped
1 deboned kid
Lard

Prepare the stuffing. Coat the bottom of a large skillet with olive oil and fry the offal briefly with the onion, salt, pepper, and parsley.

Bring a large pot of salted water to a boil and cook the vermicelli al dente, drain, and remove to a large bowl. Combine the offal with the vermicelli (amount according to the size of the kid). Add the pecorino, *caciocavallo*, prosciutto (*soppressata* or dried sausage can be substituted), and the hard-boiled eggs.

Meanwhile, prepare the kid by greasing the inner cavity with lard. Insert the prepared stuffing and sew up the cavity with kitchen twine. Grease the exterior of the kid with olive oil, sprinkle with salt and pepper, and place in a large roasting pan. Bake in a preheated 350° oven for 45 minutes. Remove from the oven, turn the kid and bake for another 45 minutes.

Church window in Randazzo

Variations

The variations are many, but not substantial. Substitute rice or macaroni for the vermicelli; grill on a spit; aromatize the exterior of the kid with crushed myrtle berries and bay leaves.

"false lean" meat ROLL
Falsumauru catanisi

This specialty is by now well-known throughout Italy, even though elsewhere and in some areas of Sicily it can be erroneously referred to as a "polpettone" (a meat loaf in Italian). The difference is that a true falsumauru *("false lean") is made from a single cut of meat, whereas a polpettone, even if it is stuffed, is formed from ground meat, and not always ground beef at that. (See the following recipe for a* purpittuni, *a meat loaf.)*

This recipe is a specialty of Catania, but there are many similar recipes throughout the island that differ only in the ingredients for the stuffing.

The name falsumauru *is derived from the fact that the dish appears to be lean on the outside, but it contains a very rich mixture of cheese and eggs inside.*

Ingredients

Slab of beef	2 tablespoons extra-virgin olive oil
1 onion, finely chopped	Sea salt
Fresh flat-leaf parsley, chopped	Pepper
2 cloves garlic, finely chopped	Red wine
3/4 to 1 cup total of *caciocavallo,* pecorino, and provolone, diced	1 tablespoon tomato paste
1/2 cup sausage, chopped	
1/4 cup mortadella, chopped	

Spread and flatten the meat with a meat pounder as if it were a large steak, keeping the shape as rectangular as possible. In a large bowl, combine the onion, garlic, cheeses, sausage, olive oil, and salt and pepper to taste. Combine thoroughly. Spread the mixture over the surface of the meat. Roll up and secure firmly—including the ends—with kitchen twine to create a log shape. In a well-oiled heavy-bottomed casserole, brown the *falsumauru* on all sides. Stir in red wine and tomato paste. Once the wine has reduced, add a little water and simmer over a low heat until cooked through.

Meatballs in Lemon Leaves Purpetti ccâ fogghia di lumìa

THIS is a typical dish throughout the Province of Catania, which probably originated in Acitrezza and Riposto. The meatballs are made from ground meat, like typical meatballs, but they are wrapped in lemon leaves and then fried.

Meat Loaf
Purpittuni

Ingredients

- 1 onion, finely sliced
- 2 cloves garlic, crushed
- Extra-virgin olive oil
- 2 tablespoons *strattu* (tomato extract) diluted with red wine
- 1 pound ground beef, plus 1 pound pork, mixed
- 1 bay leaf, crushed
- Sea salt
- Pepper
- 2 eggs, beaten
- Bread crumbs
- 4 hard-boiled eggs
- Fresh flat-leaf parsley, chopped

Coat the bottom of a skillet with olive oil and gently fry the onion and garlic until translucent. Add the tomato extract to the pan. Once this has almost evaporated, remove skillet from the heat.

In a large bowl, combine the meat, the cooled onion mixture, a bay leaf, eggs, parsley, and salt and pepper to taste. Blend thoroughly. If the mixture is too wet, add a few of tablespoons of dried bread crumbs. Form into a large loaf, inserting shelled hard-boiled eggs in the center, and place in a roasting pan. Bake in a preheated 350° oven for 1 hour.

Variations

Noteworthy variations are the following: you can use all beef, all pork, or a mixture of the two; the stuffing can be made with different ingredients and spices; and the meat loaf can be cooked in a pan until brown, instead of in the oven. You can also add tomato sauce toward the end to form a dense sauce.

roasted veal intestines
Zinènu, Zirènu e Vudèddu pappùni

The term zinènu *or* zirènu *derives from the ancient Italian word* geno, *and refers to the duodenum, small intestine. The term* vudèddu pappùni *used by Sicilian butchers is the soft fatty intestines of the calf, which are sought after by gourmets.*

Ingredients
Calf intestines
Extra-virgin olive oil
Mint leaves
Fresh basil leaves
Fresh oregano leaves
Sea salt
Pepper

Wash the intestines inside and out and cut into lengths of approximately 4 inches. Lightly oil the strips and place over moderate heat on a charcoal grill. As soon as they are browned and cooked through, coat with a mixture of olive oil, mint, basil, oregano, and salt and pepper to taste. Eat while still very hot.

The anatomy of ruminants' stomachs consists of the *rumine*, a sac where the food they eat is deposited; a second sac called *reticolo* or *cuffia* (tripes shaped like little cells) that is used to bring the food to the esophagus; a third part of the stomach called *omaso* (the *centopelli* tripe or *foglietto*) where the chewed and by now liquid food is deposited; and finally a fourth area known as *abomaso*, where digestion occurs. The chyme formed in the *abomaso* finally penetrates the small intestine, the duodenum.

View of Catania

coria

snails

LET'S TALK about snails, numerous throughout the island, appreciated by many, and prepared in many different ways. Without giving an exhaustive zoological classification, suffice it to say that Sicilians are familiar with four different families of snails, although there is some confusion regarding their dialect names in different provinces.

The very small, white-shelled snails commonly known as *babbalùci, vavalùci, cazzicàddi* and *bucalàci* belong to the first family.

The second family includes the common garden variety, generally called *vaccarèddi*, but around Catania and Messina they are also referred to as *bucalàci* (see the following recipe); around Palermo, these are also called *babbalùci.* I have included another recipe for these.

The third family includes the type of snails identified by dark brown shells and by the presence of an operculum, a retractable lid that closes the shell. It is known by many different names in Sicilian, including: *scaùzzu, izzu, munachèddi, 'ntuppatèddi, scataddìzzi*, etc.

Finally, the fourth family includes the *vignaiola* or *martinaccio* types, which are greenish-brown and are the largest of them all. The most common dialect names are *barbàniu, crastùni,* and *muntùni.*

ROasTeD snaiLs
Bucalàci arrustùti

To avoid repetition, it must be said once and for all that before any preparation, snails must be "purged," or left without food other than perhaps a leaf of lettuce or some bran, for at least 3 days. They are then rinsed thoroughly and boiled before using any other method of preparation. This is because once they come out of dormancy, they nibble at anything around and may ingest vegetation that may not be toxic to them but that can be harmful to humans. The exception to this rule are snails sold with closed operculum (the white membrane over their opening, as these snails have purged themselves before going into hibernation).

Ingredients
Snails
Extra-virgin olive oil
Sea salt
Pepper

After washing them thoroughly, place the snails on a hot grill for approximately 10 minutes. Transfer to a bowl and dress with abundant olive oil, salt and pepper. Traditionally the snails are sucked out of their shells and are eaten with the hands.

Frog Soup
Larunci a suppitedda

The reader might be surprised to discover a recipe for frogs, well-known in other regions, but almost unknown in Sicily. But there is a tradition in one area—around Paternò—where the use of frogs goes far into the distant past and documentation proves that the entire area was once a swamp, and therefore the natural habitat of frogs. So, out of hunger or acquired taste, the inhabitants developed different ways of preparing them. Their names in Sicilian are larunchi, laurunchi, giurane, *and finally* pisci-cantànnu, *from a fable that speaks of them as "singing fish."*

Ingredients
    Frogs' legs
    Extra-virgin olive oil for deep frying
    2 cloves garlic, finely sliced
    Fresh flat-leaf parsley, chopped
    Sea salt
    Pepper
    Juice from 1 lemon

In a heavy-bottomed pot, quickly fry the frogs' legs, without flouring or anything else added, in boiling olive oil. Drain on paper towels.

In a large skillet, gently fry garlic until transluscent in olive oil, then add the frogs' legs, parsley, salt and pepper to taste, and a little water. Cook for 20 minutes after bringing to a boil. Reduce the cooking liquid, add a few drops of lemon over the frogs' legs, and serve.

ARTICHOKES

AS we know, artichokes were commonly known to the Romans. Columella records them with the name *cinara*. It is not known why they were not cultivated for some time. It is a fact that during the late medieval period they were imported in large quantities from Ethiopia and in the 15th and 16th centuries appeared in Tuscany. The artichoke found an ideal habitat in Sicily and its cultivation has continued producing enormous quantities everwhere on the island, with special varieties grown around Palermo and in the Caltanissetta area. The dialect names are diverse and strange-sounding —*cacocciula, cacuocciuli, carciofala*—and the recipes are almost infinite. We will include a few of them from other provinces. The following recipe includes anchovies, *anciovi*, which are the main ingredient for the stuffing.

It is not necessary to spend much time discussing the method of initial preparation of the artichokes themselves. If they are to be cooked stuffed or roasted on a grill, they are left whole; if they are to be prepared in some kind of sauce, only a few tough external leaves are removed and the extreme tips of the leaves cut. Finally, if one wishes to prepare a dish of only the artichoke hearts, almost all the external leaves are removed as well as the internal "choke" in the very center.

Peeled artichokes have a tendency to oxidize in the open air, which is why it is recommended that they be plunged immediately in a bowl of cold water and a few drops of lemon juice as each one is prepared, taking care not to overdo the lemon juice as too strong a lemon flavor may not be compatible with other ingredients.

coria

ARTICHOKES WITH ANCHOVIES
Cacuocciuli cu l'anciovi

Ingredients
　　Artichokes

　　Stuffing amounts for each serving
　　2 tablespoons bread crumbs
　　2 tablespoons pecorino with peppercorns
　　2 cloves garlic, chopped
　　Fresh flat-leaf parsley, chopped
　　2 salted anchovy fillets, chopped
　　Extra-virgin olive oil
　　Sea salt

Choose large artichokes with stems. Remove a few rows of the tougher outer leaves. Stand them upside down and, holding their stems, beat them on a marble slab until the artichokes open.*

Prepare the stuffing for each artichoke. Mix bread crumbs, pecorino, garlic, parsley, anchovy fillets, then add salt to taste and enough oil to moisten the stuffing. Stuff each artichoke making sure to fill the entire cavity as much as possible. After cutting off the stems, place artichokes side-by-side in a large saucepan with a lid, drizzle the center of each with a little olive oil, and add a few inches of water to the bottom of the pan. Cover and simmer for at least 30 minutes on a low flame, making sure that the pan does not boil dry, at least until the very final moment.

*Many Italian varieties do not have "chokes." If using artichokes with "chokes," they must be removed at this point, before stuffing.

FRIED EGGPLANT WITH BéCHAMEL SAUCE
Milinciani sciatri e matri

The name of this dish is more interesting than the recipe itself, even though it is the first time, perhaps the only time, we encounter the use of béchamel in recipes.

Ingredients
> Eggplants
> Sea salt
> Béchamel sauce
> Nutmeg
> 2 eggs, beaten
> Bread crumbs
> Extra-virgin olive oil

Slice unpeeled eggplants into thin discs, sprinkle with salt and set aside until the liquid has seeped out. Rinse and pat dry with paper towels. Set out a plate of bread crumbs. Spread one slice with béchamel sauce (see below) and a pinch of nutmeg and cover with a second slice. Dip these first in the beaten eggs, then in the bread crumbs until coated.

Deep-fry the "sandwiches" in boiling olive oil in a heavy-bottomed pot until they attain a deep golden brown. Drain quickly, sprinkle with salt, and serve immediately.

Simple béchamel sauce: in a small saucepan, whisk 2 tablespoons of melted butter with 2 tablespoons flour, then slowly whisk in 1 cup of milk until producing a sauce with a thick creamy consistency.

This strange Arabic term, *sciatri e matri*, little known to Sicilians themselves, is derived from Syrian Arabic. It was imported by the Turks with the sound of *ciatra-patra*, which expresses an exclamation of surprise or disdain. Mortillaro's dictionary follows the same line of meaning defining it as "an interjection denoting disdain or admiration." In our case, therefore, it signifies "a dish that evokes marvel." Another dictionary by Traina, however, explains that the expression means a *container of farts* which justifies this time the interjection of disdain, or a *piritera*, an instrument that was used once to avoid bad odor under the sheets.

Béchamel sauce seems to have been invented by a cook in the household of the Marquis Louis Bechameil, a nobleman thief who made his fortune during the civil war at the beginnning of Louis XIV's reign. This sauce, almost identical to the original, arrived in Sicily with the same name.

"Drowned" Broccoli
Vrocculi affucati

It is impossible to classify all the varieties of broccoli available, which are referred to in dialect with many different and colorful names, not all of which refer to an actual variety. The best way to identify which variety is intended is to describe the shape, color and flavor.

Ingredients
- 2 pounds tender baby black broccoli
- 1 onion, finely sliced
- Extra-virgin olive oil
- Sea salt
- Pepper
- 1/2 glass red wine
- 3 tablespoons pecorino with peppercorns, slivered

Clean the broccoli, removing the outside leaves, rinse, and chop roughly. Place in a saucepan with the onion, salt and pepper to taste, and a little water. Cover and simmer for 20 minutes. At this point, add a half glass of red wine and stir until the wine has almost completely evaporated. Quickly stir through the pecorino. This dish can either be served lukewarm or cold as a *contorno,* side dish, or hot as part of a second course.

Variations
Even a basic dish such as this, typical in Catania, is subject to small variations from household to household: white wine can be substituted for the red; the onion can be fried before adding the broccoli; and some people add a few chopped anchovies, or finely-chopped black olives.

CHEESE

The range of cheese available is enormous. The following is a list of only the oldest and the most typical.

Bronte was one of the three cyclops who manned the furnace of Mount Etna, to fashion Zeus' lightning and the arms of the Heroes. The other two comrades were Sterope and Piracmone. The symbolism of the name is clear: *Bronte* from the Greek is thunder; *sterope* means lightning; *pir* means fire, and *acmon is* anvil. This is how Vito Amico explains it in his *Dizionario Topografico della Sicilia.*

Bruntisi

A sheep's milk cheese with peppercorns characteristic of the town of Bronte, after which it is named. Depending on its age, it can be served soft and fresh, firm as a table cheese, or aged enough to be grated.

Lacciata o Quagghiata

This is the whey that remains after the milk has curdled (its name derives from the Provençal name *lachado,* meaning milk). You can still taste it fresh in small sheep farms early in the morning when the shepherds prepare ricotta.

Ricotta sicca

Dried ricotta is a lightly salted ricotta that has been left in the sun to dry. Quite rare and difficult to come by, it is mainly found in Paternò, near Catania, and Pollina, near Palermo.

camouflaged or nun's eggs
Ova 'ntuppatèddi, od Ova munachèddi

A curious way to call hard-boiled eggs, split in half and then prepared in such a way as to make them unrecognizable as eggs. The derivation of the name is in fact quite interesting. 'Ntuppatèddi (snails) recalls the women who used to be seen among the crowd during the Procession of Saint Agatha in Catania, who covered their heads with a silk hood with only one hole (which allowed them to see with their right eye but which made them unrecognizable as well).* The name munachèddi, which means "little nuns," is analogous to 'ntuppatèddi, probably referring to "cloistered nuns" who exist but cannot be seen.

Ingredients
> Hard-boiled eggs, shelled
> Beaten eggs
> Bread crumbs
> Extra-virgin olive oil
> Sea salt
> Tomato sauce

Set out a bowl of bread crumbs. Slice the eggs in half and dip them first in the beaten eggs, then in the bread crumbs. Fry these in a heavy-bottomed casserole or pot in hot oil until golden. Drain and salt to taste.

Prepared in this way they become part of a fritto misto (mixed fry). Usually, however, if after frying they are submerged in tomato sauce and gently warmed together for a few minutes, they are served as a second course.

*Giuseppe Pitrè (1841–1916) in *Feste patronali di Sicilia* related this custom typical of the Feast of Saint Agatha that takes place in great pomp on February 3:

". . . to hide their identities, some women wore a sort of sack made of black silk that had one hole so they could see using their right eye, and walked into the crowd in twos, threes or groups. Camouflaged as they were . . . they approached friends or acquaintances and, taking them under the arm, led them or were led by them to the pastry shop so that they could offer them some *confetti* or other delicacies they desired . . . ."

catania fruits, nuts, and sweets

fruits and nuts

THE PROVINCE of Catania is the largest producer of citrus fruit not only in Sicily but in all of Italy. Specialized areas of production vary from municipality to municipality. Biancavilla produces blood oranges, Lentini specializes in a variety known as *more,* Francofonte produces *tarocchi,* and Paternò produces oranges of every variety.

Other fruits deserve mention, many referred to in the ancient myths and legends of Sicilian folklore. There are the peaches of Adrano;[1] the cherries of Mascali; the figs from Militello Val di Catania;[2] the apples from Pedara, Pettineo, and Zafferana Etnea, and especially the *puma* of Saint Alfio,[3] a variety of small, bright yellow apples; and the pears from Milo and Pedara.[4] Prickly pears[5] *(fichi d'India)*, now becoming available nationally, are best in Belpasso, Bronte, and Militello Val di Catania.

Emerald pistachios are found in Belpasso, Bronte, Mascalucia, Paternò, and a few neighboring towns, and also in the area around Agrigento—the only parts of Sicily where this mysterious tree grows.[6] These nuts are indispensable in the preparation of many typical Sicilian desserts and sweets.

1. Plutarch related that the peach tree was dedicated to Harpocrates, the god of Silence (corresponding to the Egyptian god *har-po-crod*) who was represented as a boy with fingers on his lips. This tree was known to the Romans who imported it from the Orient, perhaps from Persia, as suggested by the name *persicum* and by the name Sicilians use for its fruit, *piersicu*. (It was not appreciated by them—Pliny, Galen, and the Salerno School of Medicine spoke of it with disdain.) In Sicily, it was cultivated intensely by the Arabs.

2. These magnificent fruits, both fresh and preserved, have satisfied and nourished countless generations and have given rise to numerous anecdotes. One came down to us from Cicero's own mouth: (*De Divinatione*). He related that in ancient times among the many varieties there was one called "figs of Cauna" (a city in Caria). While Marcus Crassus was boarding his ship at Brindisi to move against the Greeks, a vendor from the peer yelled out *cauneàs,* meaning "figs of Cauno." The diviners interpreted it as *cave ne* which means "beware of leaving," an omen of disaster. In fact Crassus was beaten. Another less famous anecdote involves a Sicilian shoemaker who was extremely jealous of his figs and worked underneath the tree to keep them

sweets

A COMPETITION to invent sweets, albeit undeclared, and an attempt to surpass one another seems to have gone on in every part of the Province of Catania. At Easter, all produce the *aceddu ccu l'ova* ("the dove with eggs inside"). This typical and highly symbolic sweet is usually modeled into the form of a little basket, a dove, or some other figure, in which eggs have been inserted. Two strips of dough forming a cross are usually used to secure the eggs to the body of the bird.

Here is a list of the treats to try, according to season and the festivals in Catania. In Bronte you will find the *filletta*, a special version of sponge cake. Giarre produces *strunzi d'ancilu* ("Angels' Droppings"), and the *amaretti di pinoli* (pine nut macaroons). In Militello you will find the *giammella*, a sponge cake glazed with icing in different colors, and the *pipirata*, an original specialty based on rice, *vinu cottu*, pine nuts, and sugar.

During the grape harvest in Paternò, we find *cudidde*, a kind of homemade vermicelli cooked in new, unfermented wine; and the famous *schiumone*, a zabaglione coated in ice cream. All over Catania there are the traditional *turruni*, nougat (*torrone* in Italian). If you want to sink your teeth into something different, try the kind produced at Linguaglossa, filled with hazelnuts. In Paternò they use almonds and pistachios, where they are made for the Feast of Saint Barbara, the local Patron Saint, and at Christmas.

There is an ancient bakery in Santa Venerina, where they prepare all the traditional sweets of Catania. If you are passing through Zafferana Etnea, you must buy some *sudda* or chestnut honey, even if the latter is not made from the famous tree known as the *castagno dei cento cavalli*.[7]

under guard. Some of his friends wanted to spite him for this and took turns passing before him, saying: "Don Paulinu, why are so so pale?" or "Why is your face so drawn and pale?"or "You must be ill, you've changed so much!" This went on until Don Paulinu, now worried, went to the doctor, leaving his fig tree unguarded, just long enough for his friends to eat all his figs.

3. They are special apples, small to medium size, with a wonderful aroma. Vendors wrap them in white paper to preserves them.

4. This was related by Pitrè, certainly not referring to a tree in Milo or Pedara. A peasant had a pear tree that did not produce any pears. The man, following tradition, warned the tree: "If you don't produce any pears next year, I will chop you down." And so it happened. The next year he cut down the tree and carved a crucifix from the wood. A bad year followed and the poor man went to pray so the next year would be better. Then his wife fell ill and the man prayed in vain for her to get well. Finally, penniless, he prayed to get good work. Nothing happened. So he picked up the crucifix and said: "I recognize you as a pear tree that produced no pears and now as a crucifix you make no miracles."

5. We note that the prickly pear, a cactus, is of Mexican and southwest American origin, arriving in Sicily after the discovery of America. Some believe that this *Opuntia* genus arrived with the Arabs, as it is listed in encyclopedias with the synonym "fig fom Barbary" [North African coast] and in England it is also called "Barbary pear." Several Sicilian legends relate that this plant was

'Nzuddi

Perhaps not even Sicilians know the actual origin of the name, which is a diminuitive of the name Vicenzu *(Vincent),* Vicinzuddu *in dialect for the singular and* Vicinzuddi *in the plural. In fact, these cookies were produced for the first time by the nuns in the Convent of San Vincenzo in Catania, and from there they became a local tradition.[8]*

Ingredients
    6 cups flour
    5 1/2 cups sugar
    1/2 ounce yeast [dissolved in lukewarm water]
    3 to 4 ounces (1/3 cup) ground, roasted almonds
    Whole almonds
    1 tablespoon candied orange peel, finely-chopped
    Ground cinnamon
    Extra-virgin olive oil

In a bowl, combine the flour, sugar, yeast (the original recipe calls for *ammoniaca per dolci,* "ammonia for sweets") almonds, orange peel and a pinch of cinnamon. Make the dough using a little warm water, sufficient to produce a light and fluffy consistency. Divide the dough and roll out into sheets. Cut out rounds similar to macaroons and press a whole almond into the center of each. Bake the cookies in batches on a greased baking sheet in a preheated 400° oven until lightly browned.

Variation

An ancient recipe listed the following ingredients: 5 cups *maiorca* [cake] flour; 4 cups sugar; 3 1/2 cups chopped almonds; 8 eggs; cinnamon and vanilla; as many uncooked almonds as the cookies.

originally poisonous and that it was brought by the Turks who wanted to exterminate the entire population, but later became a beneficial tree by miracle.

6. The pistachio tree has a trunk and branches that are contorted and can reach 10 to 12 feet in height. It is of Asiatic origin and cultivated in Persia, Syria, Palestine, Iraq, India, Russia, and in temperate zones of Africa and in California. In Sicily, it grows only in the areas of Catania and Agrigento. It is a very strange tree in that it must be grafted onto a terebinth (known as *scornabeccu*) to grow. It survives only in precise locations and it makes fruit only if a male (a tree that does not produce fruit) is positioned in such a way as to pollinate no more than eight female trees.

7. In Saint Alfio near Acireale there is a 4,000 year-old tree according to legend. It's known as the *castagno dei 100 cavalli* ("The Chestnut of the Hundred Horses"). The four trunks that grew out of the single roots reach 100 feet in height. The legend relates that under its cover, at the time of the Angevins, one hundred knights and their horses took refuge there during a storm.

8. We refer to St. Vincent de Paul who, between 1625 and 1633, founded the Lazarian and Vincentian Institutes and the congregation of the Sisters of Charity to assist abandoned children, poor women, the poor, the blind and the demented: all of this to document that the biscuits we are discussing were born in the 17th century.

Lenten Biscuits
Quaresimali

By its very name, this recipe originally guaranteed the absence of animal-based ingredients such as lard, eggs, milk, and milk derivatives, which were once entirely forbidden during Lent, as was the consumption of meat. Whoever invented the original recipe had to perform the equivalent of culinary somersaults to create a finished product that held together and tasted good without those staple ingredients. Naturally, once the degree of ecclesiastical severity was relaxed, the original recipes were gradually altered and lard and eggs crept in and, as usual, hundreds of variations sprang up. This is one of those variations, typical of the Catania area.

Ingredients
- 1 1/2 cups flour
- 2 pounds (4 cups) lightly-roasted almonds, roughly chopped
- 5 cups sugar
- 6 whole eggs

In a mixing bowl, work together the flour, almonds, sugar and eggs, adding enough water to make a workable dough. Divide the dough and roll out into long rolls about 1 1/2 inches thick. Place the rolls on a greased baking sheet and leave overnight.

The next day, bake in a preheated 350° oven for about 20 minutes. Remove from the oven, and, while still hot, slice into rounds. Place the rounds on baking sheets, and return to the oven to cook until done.

Variations

Regional variations differ only in regard to the quantities and ingredients. The method of preparation is identical. Around Palermo and Enna, the recipe calls for 2 cups flour, about 5 cups sugar, about 4 cups almonds, 1/2 cup lard, orange peel, and cinnamon. In Siracusa, it calls for 6 egg whites raher than whole eggs.

chocolate "salami"
Salami Turcu

This cookie is called salame *for its long (biscotti) shape. This old recipe was invented to use cookies that have become a little stale. The collective imagination associated chocolate with dark skin.*

Ingredients
    1 pound (2 cups) assorted crumbled biscotti
    1 egg, beaten
    1/2 cup sugar
    Walnut-sized piece of butter, melted
    2 ounces (1/4 cup) dark chocolate, melted
    Milk

In a mixing bowl, combine crumbled biscotti, egg, sugar, butter, and chocolate (bitter cocoa powder can be substituted). Add enough milk to form a firm paste, then form it into a long sausage shape. Place the roll obtained in the refrigerator to firm. Once it has set, remove from the refrigerator, slice and serve.

Variations
One can add all manner of extra ingredients such as raisins, pistachios, diced candied peel, chopped almonds (if there are no almond biscotti in the ingredients).

rice-filled fritters
Sfinciteddi

Quite rare today, this very old recipe for little fritters are characteristic of the Catania area.

Ingredients
    2 cups rice
    Milk
    1 cup sugar
    Zest of 2 oranges
    Flour
    Yeast
    Lard
    Melted honey
    Cinnamon

In a large pot, boil the rice in milk until cooked then drain and transfer to a mixing bowl. Combine with the sugar and the orange peel. Meanwhile, prepare a dough with the flour and yeast. Once the dough has risen, roll out into very thin sheets and cut out 4-inch circles. Place a tablespoon of rice mixture on each. Fold over and seal the edges as for preparing ravioli. In a heavy-bottomed pot, deep-fry in hot fat until the fritters are golden, and then drain on paper towels. Before serving, drizzle them with melted honey and a dusting of cinnamon.

Hens' Droppings, Angels' Droppings, Queen's Biscuits
Strunzi di sciocca, Strunzi d'ancilu, Viscotta Regina

These poor cookies have a rather vulgar name – "Hens' Droppings" – mainly because of their shape and the obvious parallel. It can be presumed that a group opposed to the clergy then changed the name to "Angels' Droppings." Among more sophisticated households, the name was made more respectable by changing it to "The Queen's Biscuits," although we suspect that they were alluding to something analogous, only royal this time.

Ingredients
    6 cups flour
    1 cup sugar
    Zest of 1 lemon
    1 ounce yeast, dissolved in a little warm water
    Lard
    Sesame seeds

In a mixing bowl, prepare a dough with the flour, sugar, lemon peel and yeast. Knead until smooth and elastic and leave in a warm place for a few of hours until it has risen. Knead the dough a second time, divide it, and form these into the rough shape of large *grissini* bread sticks. Cut these into 2- to 3-inch lengths and roll each in the sesame seeds to coat the exterior. Place on a greased baking sheet and bake in a preheated 350° oven until crisp.

Variations

In some cases, after removing from the oven, they are tossed, while still hot, in a glaze of sugar and lemon extract or a melted chocolate glaze.

Tatù

Typical cookies found all along the Ionian coast.

Ingredients
  6 cups flour
  2 pounds (4 cups) raw almonds, peeled then ground to a powder
  5 cups sugar
  1 3/4 cups sugar for the syrup
  4 ounces (1/2 cup) dark cooking chocolate

In a large mixing bowl, combine the flour, almonds, and sugar, with a little warm water to make a dough. Form small balls from this dough and place on a greased baking sheet. Bake in a preheated 350° oven for approximately 20 minutes.

Meanwhile, in a large pot, prepare a syrup by dissolving the sugar in 1 cup of water, and adding the chocolate once this boils.

Remove the cookies from the oven and, while hot, toss them in the chocolate syrup and set them out to cool.

Little Olives of Saint Agatha Uliveddi di Sant' Aita

THESE sweets are called Little Olives of Saint Agatha after the Patron Saint of Catania. According to traditional folklore, the Saint, while being led to her martyrdom, stopped to tie her sandal at a place where an olive tree miraculously sprang up. Hence the tradition of preparing sweets shaped like little olives from almond paste, the same that is used for the "frutti di Martorana." These little Olives of Saint Agatha are the traditional pastel green.

wines

THere is one *Denominazione di Origine Controllata (DOC)* wine, or Wine of Designated Origin, in the Catania area, named *Etna*. It is produced in the form of *bianco,* white wine with eleven and one-half percent alcohol content, a *bianco superiore* with twelve percent alcohol content, and *rosso,* red, and rosé with twelve and one-half percent alcohol content. *Etna* is produced in twenty municipalities in Catania. The vineyards bottling this wine are Martinella, Marticino, Montedolce, Murgo, Ragabo, Rampante, Realvini, Rocca d'Alpi, Rusvini, Solicchiata, Torrepalino, and Villagrande.

The Italian government has identified and awarded the DOC to unique and significant wines in specific regions or towns. Their geographical origin determines quality and particular characteristics.

Few table wines are produced in the rest of the area but among the most notable are the red and rosé *Fuoco dell'Etna*, "fire of Mount Etna," the white and red *Imakara,* and the *Tenuta di San Michele.* The sparkling wine called *Murgo* is produced according to the classic method.

Liqueurs

Several distilleries produce liqueurs and spirits, including the classic *Amaro d'Etna.*

SURROUNDED by the sea, Siracusa cannot help but have what is called locally *cucina dello scoglio*, "reef cuisine," a tradition that favors the use of fresh and salted fish and seafood. The island Ortigia, the ancient heart of the city, holds the mythical Arethusa Fountain in whose waters many species of fish swim, caress the spirits of its two lovers,[1] and provide a hint of Siracusa's delicious fish recipes.

Among the finest of the regional pasta dishes are *pasta a sirausana* and *ccâ muddica*, pasta Siracusa-style and with bread crumbs; and *pasta ccâ buttàrica*, pasta with tuna roe. Regional dishes such as ricotta and sausages *(rigatuna ccâ ricotta e sausizza)* survive, and Palazzolo Acreide is well-known for *maccarunna* with walnuts, a traditional devotional dish for All Saints' Day, and *taccuna di mulinu* ("millers' heels"). Siracusan homemade pastas are dressed in a variety of ways.[2]

The renowned seafood specialties owe their reputation not to the use of the most expensive fish available, but to quite the opposite: the most modest species such as *rummu* (brill), *vopi, sicci, pisci capuni, razza* (ray), and *squatru* (angel shark); and a huge variety of smaller species, first among them the *minchia*, shore rockling.[3]

Every day in the tranquil city of Siracusa, among its wealth of ancient buildings and ruins, an outdoor market is set up offering a bewildering array of regional food, including a

particular green-skinned Siracusan lemon, almonds from Avola (the very best for making sugared almonds), baked ricotta (becoming rare these days), robustly flavored salted tuna sold in pieces, and salted sardines prepared at Vindicari and Marzamemi.

The presence of a wide variety of cultivated and wild vegetables testifies to the area's long agricultural tradition. Inland, Siracusans, not having access to fresh seafood, long ago invented the art of breeding freshwater fish—continuing the ancient tradition of fishing their lakes and rivers and creating notable specialties such as the *trota ccâ niputedda*,[4] trout with catmint.

Typical meat dishes are few although the people of Siracusa are very fond of sausage no matter how it's prepared, and they eat it in winter once it has dried out. (The best comes from Palazzolo Acreide.)

Great consumers of snails, Siracusans are experts at preparing them and it appears that they invented the recipe for *scaüzzi o 'ntuppattieddi 'mbriachi*,[5] ("drunken snails").

Confectionary has a very strong tradition in Siracusa and the truly traditional sweets are based on almonds and dried fruit, such as *schiumette*, *dolci di mennula* (almond sweets), *bocconotti*, *turruni* (nougats) and *viscotta rizzi*[6] (curly biscuits). Throughout the region we find *pastifuorti*, made of a typical dough strongly flavored with cinnamon cloves that is

View of Ortigia's strand

1. According to the myth, Alpheus hopelessly loved a nymph named Arethusa who, to get away from him, fled to Siracusa where she was changed into a spring. The persistent Alpheus, however, changed himself into a river and, traveling beneath the Ionian Sea without having his fresh water mixing with sea water, emerged in Ortigia at the spring to join with the waters of his beloved. In ancient times, the spring was dedicated to the goddess Diana and no one dared touch the many fish that teemed in it. Fishermen departing on long journeys would take along some of the spring water, which they considered more "long-lasting" than water from any other source. This spring is well-preserved to this day, bordered by tall papyrus, and is believed to have been formed from the union of two star-crossed lovers.

2. A special Siracusan fresh homemade pasta (now difficult to find) is prepared with 6 cups flour, 3 eggs, and no salt. Knead the dough and flatten it, cutting it into strips then into little squares of 1/2 inch. With an appropriate tool, roll the square and allow it to dry. Women who have skilled experience can roll 4 to 5 squares at a time.

3, *Squatru,* angel shark. (known as "damsel") deserves a special note. Although its meat is tasty and has few bones, it would not receive much attention except for the very strange names given to it along the coastline such as: *minchia di re*, *pizzi di re* (King's points), *cazzurri*, *viriola,* etc. It measures less than 10 inches and has long orange stripes and multicolored hints. Perhaps it was given a royal and virile name because of its shape, beauty and length.

4. *Niputedda* (catmint) is an aromatic herb not used much in gastronomy (only to add flavor to some fresh water fish or to add aroma to the water when whole figs, known as *passuluni,* are immersed before they are dried in the sun). The herb was widely used in popular medicine because people believed that its use could alleviate nerve spasms. In Sicilian legends, Saint Anne was said to have drunk a beverage made from it at the time of Mary's birth, and Mary herself chewed a few leaves of it at the death of Jesus.

5. *Scaùzzi* is one of the many names by which snails are known in Sicilian, especially the ones that have a dark brown shell with an operculum, the white membrane that closes the opening. The etymology is found in the root for slave, *scau,* and the diminutive *scauzzi,* little slaves, which the collective imagination associated with the brown color of the skin of slaves.

6. *Mennula* means almond and *viscotta ricci* mean curly biscuits.

7. *Pastifuorti* refers to cinnamon-flavored dough common to all Sicilian pastries. Whoever invented the technique for preparing this specialty deserves a prize. It consists of a mixture of flour and sugar flavored with cinnamon cloves that is allowed to dry overnight. The following day one moistens only the bottom of the shaped biscuits. When these are placed in the oven almost all the sugar melts and forms the base of the biscuit while the top remains pale, clear, and hollow. Thus inventing the *ossi di morto* ("dead man's bones") was easy. The mixture was cut in the desired shape and when the biscuit finished baking, it reflected the cook's intentions.

8. The *mustata* (*mostardo* in Italian) is a totally different product from the one prepared with mustard in northern Italy. In Sicily it refers to wine must (grape juice) boiled to prevent fermentation. After it's clarified and filtered, vanilla and orange skins are added. Finally it is made into a pudding with the addition of starch or semolina. The pudding is then enriched with toasted almonds and placed in special molds that are exposed to the sun. After a few days the pudding is taken out of the molds and allowed to dry in the sun completely. *Mustata* is stored in cans or containers for consumption during the winter months by children, as snacks, or for desserts. *Mustata* can be made also of prickly pear juice or mixing grape and prickly pear juice.

9. *Cuccìa* became a

traditional dish for the Feast Day of Saint Lucy as the following legend has passed on to us. Siracusa was suffering a period of famine and everyone prayed for its end. On December 13th (the Patron Saint's feast day) a ship appeared loaded with wheat arrived in the port. The starving people, unwilling to wait for the wheat to be milled, decided to eat it right away by boiling it. The tradition of preparing *cuccìa,* and eating nothing else for the entire day, was born to commemorate that miraculous event.

10. Sesames or anything made with sesame is called *giuggiulèna* or *cubbaita* in Sicily. Here we would like to point out that sesame was widely used among the Egyptians, Phoenicians, Greeks, and Romans, not only as a source of an oil used in cosmetics, but also as something added to foods. In Greece, sesame seeds were added to cheese to create the *sesamotyron,* as Strabo recorded; it was mixed with rue to obtain the *sesamotyrpagès* mentioned in the *Batracomiomachia;* and it was added to

bread and to pizza, according to Filosseno. The sesame desserts in Sicily are the heirs of a very ancient Greek specialty known as *mylloi,* which had the form of a female pubis and was made in October in honor of the goddess Demeter (the feasts were known as *Tesmoforie* from the name of the goddess, *Thesmophora,* the Law Giver). The feasts became traditional in Sicily during the period of Hellenic colonization.

11. No period of our civilization exists in which the honey from the Iblei Mountains has not been praised, described, and celebrated by the likes of Apuleius, Celio Rodigino, Dioscorides Pedanio, Strabo, Pliny, and Virgil. Boccone in his *Museo di piante rare* says among other things that "the honey from the Iblei Mountains manages to be better than any other honey in Italy. It's collected three times a year, in July and August, when it has the taste and aroma of thyme, and in September, when it has the smell of calamint."

shaped into bones for the traditional All Souls' Day cookies called *ossi di morti,* "dead man's bones."[7] This particular dough is also formed into the shapes of flowers or figures for Christmas. Buscemi specializes in *sacchiteddi,* called *ciascuna* at Palazzolo Acreide, which are none other than *nucatuli.* Widespread also is *cutugnata,* a wonderful quince marmelade the color of old gold, and *mustata,* a pudding made from grape must dried in the sun.[8] *Cuccìa,*[9] the obligatory devotional dish for the feast of Saint Lucy, also originates from Siracusa, as does *giuggiulèna,*[10] crispy fritters with sesame seeds, which have remained unchanged over the centuries from their Greek and Latin origins. And as we are recalling the past, beekeepers continue to produce the honey from the Iblei Mountains, celebrated by ancient writers.[11] The best today are from Melilli and Floridia.

Even the varieties of ice cream and sorbet from Syracuse are astonishing, as the versions produced here differ from the rest of the island due to the incorporation of unusual ingredients—jasmine ice cream, carob flour ice cream, black mulberry granita (a form of "ices" made with crushed ice and flavoring), and even a granita of ricotta.

Temple of Apollo ruins, Ortigia

saint joseph's day soup
Maccu di San Giuseppe, o Ministredda

This maccu *is a special soup that includes a variety of dried vegetables and beans cooked together. The recipe, which exists in various forms in other areas, fulfills a precise need—to use the vegetables not consumed during the winter. The Feast of Saint Joseph on March 19, at the beginning of spring, offers the best occasion for using the leftover vegetables.*

Ingredients

>About 1/3 cup each: dried fava beans, peas, kidney beans, and chickpeas soaked for 12 hours
>Sea salt
>Dried lentils
>Chopped borage
>Wild fennel (baby fennel leaves can be substituted)
>1 onion, finely sliced
>1 tablespoon sundried tomatoes, mashed
>*Peperoncino,* hot red chili pepper, sliced [or dried flakes] to taste
>Extra-virgin olive oil

Rinse and drain the soaked beans. Put the beans into a saucepan with enough water to cover, salt to taste, and bring to a boil. Then simmer at low heat for 1 hour. At this point, add the lentils, borage, fennel, onion, sun dried tomatoes, and some chili, and continue to cook for another hour. Taste for seasoning and drizzle with olive oil before serving.

pasta with dried tuna roe
Pasta ccâ buttarica

Buttarica (bottarga in Italian) is the sac containing the roe of the female tuna. If the sac is taken before the eggs have been deposited it is larger and richer in taste, thus more expensive. In this state, it is called bottarga di andata, *meaning that it is "on the way to" depositing the eggs. On the other hand, if it is taken after the eggs have been laid, when it usually contains fewer eggs and is leaner, it is known as* bottarga di ritorno, *or "returning bottarga." The taste, however, remains the same.*

Considering that the tuna fishing industry, as everyone knows, is associated with the area of Trapani, some people may wonder why this recipe is included as typical of Siracusa. In the area around Marzamemi and Vindicari (near Cape Passero, on the southernmost tip of Sicily) there existed equally famous tunnu, *now long forgotten, where tuna-fishing and packing were the main local industry.*

This recipe is very typical in many towns of Sicily.

Ingredients
> 1 teaspoon *buttarica (bottarga)* per serving
> Extra-virgin olive oil
> 1 pound spaghetti
> Fresh flat-leaf parsley, chopped

Grate *buttarica,* enough for each serving, and make a dressing using olive oil. Meanwhile, bring a large pot of water to a boil and cook the spaghetti until al dente. Drain and transfer to a serving platter. Dress the spaghetti with the *buttarica* and oil mixture, sprinkle with parsley and serve.

Buttarica (bottarga) can be found in specialty food markets. It comes in chunks that can be grated.

Variations
Instead of blending the uncooked *buttarica* in olive oil at room temperature, it can be added to hot olive oil in a skillet and left to heat through briefly before adding to the spaghetti. In some cases, more grated *buttarica* can be added directly to the dish, but this is a question of personal taste, as more *buttarica* will result in a much stronger taste.

PASTA WITH BREAD CRUMBS AND PASTA SIRACUSA-STYLE
Pasta ccâ 'muddica e Pasta a sirausana

The word 'muddica in the title refers to the soft crustless part of bread. It is this ingredient together with the salted anchovies that distinguishes this dish from others. The variation— Pasta a sirausana—identifies this dish as originating in Siracusa (not to be confused with another dish of the same name that appears among the dessert recipes). While pasta with bread crumbs exists everywhere on the island, the recipe from Siracusa is by far the richest and most original.

Ingredients
   2 salted anchovies per serving
   1 tablespoon extra-virgin olive oil per serving
   Peperoncino, hot red chili pepper, sliced [or dried flakes] to taste
   2 to 3 tablespoons soft pieces of crustless bread, torn
   1 pound spaghetti

Rinse the salt off the anchovies and scale them. In a skillet, fry them in olive oil then break them down with a fork, removing all fine bones where possible. Add a few flakes of chili according to taste for a spicier dish.

In a separate skillet, roast the bread pieces in a little olive oil over low heat, stirring frequently with a wooden spoon to prevent burning until they are sufficiently brown, like the color of a "monk's habit."

Meanwhile, bring a large pot of salted water to a boil and cook the spaghetti until al dente. Drain and transfer to a serving platter. Dress the spaghetti with the anchovy and oil mixture, adding more olive oil if required, then sprinkle roasted bread over each serving.

Pasta a sirausana

The preparation is analogous, but after breaking down the anchovies in a saucepan add chopped garlic, parsley, chili, and pitted green olives. The cooked and drained pasta is then transferred to the saucepan and tossed with its contents until coated. As above, the toasted bread is sprinkled on top of each portion.

Baccalà frittu

A typical dish served on Christmas Eve, originally from Augusta, but common everywhere.

Ingredients
  1 baccalà, (salted cod) presoaked and dried
  Flour for dusting
  Extra-virgin olive oil
  Fresh flat-leaf parsley, chopped
  Sea salt
  Juice of 1 lemon

Set out a plate of flour for dusting. Cut the fish into pieces, dust with flour, and fry in a skillet in the olive oil until golden. Sprinkle with salt and parsley to taste and the juice of a lemon.

Variation
In some families, the fish pieces are first dipped in egg and then flour.

Tuna semen
Lattumi di tunnu

Lattumi is the dialect word for the seminal fluid of the male tuna which it deposits over the eggs laid by the female to fertilize them. Modern science has shown that this fluid—a veritable reservoir of hormones—gives "virile" energy to those who consume it. Perhaps this explains why Sicilians have been so fond of "aphrodisiacs," even though—obviously—they did not know the scientific evidence that has emerged only now. (It might be useful to conduct a study on how food influences people's character traits.)

Ingredients
  Tuna semen
  Flour for dusting
  1 egg, beaten

1 clove garlic, finely chopped
Fresh flat-leaf parsley, chopped
Sea salt
Pepper
Extra-virgin olive oil

Lattumi looks like a whitish gelatinous mass. Wash and parboil in lightly salted water. Drain on paper towels and cut into thin slices. Set out a plate of flour and lightly dust the pieces. Combine the beaten egg, garlic, parsley, and salt and pepper to taste. Dip each slice into this batter. In a skillet, fry the slices in hot oil until golden brown.

POACHED BRILL
Rummu a stimpirata

The ingredients for this recipe are used not only in the preparation of fish, but also for meat dishes, and there are very few variations—none of which are significant—on the basic recipe. The following is typical of the Siracusa area.

Ingredients
Sliced brill, about 2 pounds
Flour for dusting
Extra-virgin olive oil
1 onion, sliced
1 heart celery including tender green leaves, finely chopped
2 garlic cloves, smashed and chopped
2 tablespoons salted capers, rinsed
12 pitted green olives
A few mint leaves
Sea salt
Pepper
White wine vinegar

Dust the fish slices in flour and fry in a skillet briefly in very hot olive oil. Remove the fish, sprinkle with salt and set aside. Lower the heat and, in the same oil, fry the onion until transparent. Add the celery heart and leaves, garlic, capers, olives, mint leaves, and salt and pepper to taste. Stir well to combine, then add the fried fish slices and shake the pan occasionally to loosen. Add a half glass of wine vinegar, cover, and simmer for about 20 minutes.

PICKEREL WITH GARLIC
Spicari all'agghiata

Here is another example of how fish in peasant cookery can have excellent results despite humble beginnings. I am referring to pickerel. I take this opportunity to reiterate that agghiata *is one of the most remarkable creations of Sicilian cuisine. The garlic's pungent flavor masks any "gamey" taste, exalts more insipid flavors, and enhances any other ingredient that may be added. It can therefore be used with any type or quality of fish.*

Ingredients
>   Pickerel, or any small fish
>   Extra-virgin olive oil
>   2 garlic cloves, chopped, per fish
>   2 tablespoons wine vinegar per fish
>   Sea salt

Clean, wash, and dry the fish thoroughly. In a large skillet, fry the fish directly in hot olive oil until done on one side. After turning, add garlic. Once this is done, add wine vinegar and allow this to evaporate completely.

Variations

A variation on the recipe involves preparing the garlic separately, frying it in olive oil until just golden, then adding the wine vinegar and cooking until partially evaporated. This mixture is added to the fish frying in another skillet, and then the fish continue cooking until the wine vinegar has evaporated.

Garlic is the king of Sicilian cooking (the onion is the queen). It is abundantly used probably because of its properties —and magic powers attributed to it over time. It was believed to be an antidote against poisons, dog bites, wasps' stings, as well as against vampires and the devil. It can lower blood pressure, cure intestinal and nefritic colics; and alleviate colds; and it is considered a vermifuge.

ANGEL SHARK MARINARA
Squatru a matalotta

Matalotta, derived from the French a la matelote, means alla marinara (mariner style) beyond the Alps and invariably requires the inclusion of red or white wine. In fact, the Sicilian matalotta has nothing to do with mariners or with the French Marine Forces, neither in regard to the technique or the ingredients!

This recipe is suitable for any strongly-flavored, firm-fleshed fish such as the squatru, palummu *(dogfish), and* razza *(ray) and others as it softens its gamey taste.*

Ingredients
> Extra-virgin olive oil
> 1 onion very thinly sliced
> 2 cloves garlic, thinly sliced
> 12 pitted green olives
> 1 tablespoon salted capers, rinsed
> Fresh flat-leaf parsley, chopped
> A few fresh basil leaves
> Tomato sauce, several cups
> Sea salt
> 2 pounds firm-fleshed fish, thinly sliced

In a large skillet, gently fry the onion in oil until golden, then add the garlic. After a few minutes, add olives, capers, parsley, basil, tomato sauce, and salt to taste. Mix well to combine and once the mixture comes to a boil, carefully add the fish slices, cover and simmer for 20 to 25 minutes on low heat.

Variations

There are some who do not use a tomato sauce already made, only chunks of ripe tomatoes. In this case, cook the dish for 10 minutes before adding the fish. Others use black olives, rather than green. Finally others add half a glass of wine vinegar before adding the tomato sauce and the raw tomatoes.

FISH SOUP SIRACUSA-STYLE
Suppa a sirausana

This is the only fish soup I shall present in this collection of regional recipes, not because it is better than the others, or because the others are inferior, but because fish soup in Sicily has never been canonized, nor has it ever had the prominence it now has in restaurants, either nationally or on the island.

The reason is quite simple. Fish soup was born among fishermen who selected the more costly fish to sell or pack for the fish market and were left with some isolated fish, unfamiliar species that could evoke skepticism among the buyers—and other little fish, the so-called fragagghia *that was too small to sell. It was a stroke of genius that inspired the fishermen to toss all the leftover fish into a soup in which they could dunk their bread. And so soup was born. It was all intuitive and logical that since the ingredients were so different in quantity and quality, this did not lead to the emergence of a preparation technique. The taste, the flavor, and the smell were different each time according to what was caught that day.*

Ingredients
Extra-virgin olive oil
4 cloves garlic, chopped
1 celery heart, chopped
Fresh flat-leaf parsley, chopped
2 tablespoons salted capers, rinsed
Pepper
Bay leaf
1 tomato, peeled, seeded and chopped
4 pounds mixed fish, including squid, baby octopus, calamari, and assorted shellfish

Pour a glass of olive oil in a terracotta pot or large heavy-bottomed pot and add the garlic, celery heart, parsley, capers, pepper, bay leaf, and tomato to add color. Place the fish on top and add what you have handy of small shellfish, sea crabs, mollusks, and the like. Pour water over the top to barely cover the seafood, bring to a boil, lower heat and simmer for 30 minutes. The real *suppa* is served!

It is very different today. Across Italy, recently the trend has been to use all kinds of high-quality fish varieties that are actually unsuitable for cooking in broth. Worse still, frozen fish is widely used and worse than that the very scent and taste of the sea is entirely lacking: the small mollusks and fish "odds and ends" that make each batch of soup different from another. Also, some restaurant chefs add exotic ingredients such as curry, saffron and so on, or overpowering spices like too much chili, which are entirely out of place in regional Sicilian cooking and are more an excuse to conceal their inept culinary skills. That is how fish soups have become canonized today and, to add insult to injury, the prices they command are inflated shamefully everywhere with rare exceptions.

RIVER TROUT WITH CATMINT
Trota du manghisi ccâ niputedda

There are many freshwater rivers and streams that flow throughout the length and breadth of Sicily. We would like to mention the Manghisi River (which is called the Cassibile when it reaches the plains of Siracusa) especially because of its connection to Pietro Mascagni, the composer, whose reputation for being buona forchetta *("a good fork," a gourmet) is not well known. The Maestro often held rehearsals for "Cavalleria Rusticana" at Noto, and his favorite dish was the trout from this river.*

Ingredients

Freshwater trout, one per serving
1 tablespoon extra-virgin olive oil per fish
1 tablespoon water
1 medium tomato, peeled, seeded, and chopped

1 clove garlic, quartered
6 salted capers, rinsed
Sea salt
A few catmint leaves

Clean the trout, wash them, and parboil in a large pan for a few minutes in boiling water with a few sprigs of catmint. Drain the fish and put them in a large skillet. Add the olive oil, water, tomato, garlic, capers, salt to taste, and catmint. Stir, heat and serve.

Variations

Some prefer to rinse the trout in wine vinegar rather than parboil them first. Others substitute a myrtle sprig for the catmint.

Vopi

What is called *vopi* in Sicily and is known as *boga* in Italy is a species of fish similar to mackerel or hake, but which has a more delicately textured flesh. Its dialect name comes from the word for ox, due to its large round, almost bovine eyes. It is highly prized for its own sake, especially in Siracusa, where no special method of preparation exists. Normally it is dusted with flour and simply fried.

poached rabbit
Cunigghiu a stimpirata

Originally this recipe was for wild rabbit or hare, but it can be used for domestic or commercially-raised rabbit.

Ingredients
3 pound rabbit, skinned, cleaned, deboned
A glass of extra-virgin olive oil
Chopped celery heart
1 parsnip, diced
2 tablespoons salted capers, rinsed
20 green olives, roughly chopped
3 cloves garlic, chopped
1 glass wine vinegar mixed with 1 teaspoon sugar
Sea salt

Cut the rabbit into relatively small pieces and in fry them in hot olive oil until they take color. Drain on paper towels. In a heavy-bottomed casserole, add a glass of olive oil, the celery heart, garlic, parsnip, capers, olives, and pieces of fried rabbit.

Combine all ingredients thoroughly and bring to a boil. Once this begins to cook, add wine vinegar with sugar, and salt to taste. Stir through to make sure all the meat comes in contact with the wine vinegar. Cover, lower the heat and simmer for 1 hour, making sure to add a little water as the liquid is absorbed or evaporates.

Variation
The base recipe is the one we just described. Over time however, local variations included the addition of tomato paste, parsley, tomato, and the elimination of garlic. Carrots were also substituted for parsnips.

Rabbits and hare have nearly disappeared because of intense cultivation of land and relentless hunting. Once when they were abundant everywhere in Sicily, it was perhaps the only good source of meat available to the poor, through poaching and nets. When I was a child, so many animals were caught during the hunt that we did not know how to cook them all. My grandmother then invented "hare meatballs."

liver "in the net"
Ficatu nno 'ntrigghiu

'Ntrigghiu or riticedda are the dialect words meaning "net." They refer to the fibrous membrane taken from a pig's abdomen that resembles a net.

Ingredients
> Pork liver plus abdominal membrane
> Sea salt
> Pepper
> 1 onion thinly sliced
> Bay leaves
> Extra-virgin olive oil

When purchasing the pork liver, ask the butcher for the abdominal membrane. Cut the liver into large pieces.

Meanwhile, plunge the membrane into a pot of boiling water for a few minutes so that it becomes more elastic. Spread it out on a work surface and cut it into pieces large enough to go around each of the liver pieces. Salt and pepper the liver pieces and wrap them in the pieces of membrane.

If using a spit, the wrapped pieces of liver are threaded onto skewers, alternating with a thin slice of onion and a bay leaf. The skewers can be set up over a moderate coal fire. If not using a grill, finely chop the onion and the bay leaves and add a small portion inside each "packet" as you make them. Fry the liver packets in a skillet.

christmas pie
Pastizzu di Natali

This pie seems to have its origins at Noto (although others claim it is from Pachino) and is in any case traditional at Christmas. That would justify the elaborate recipe.

Ingredients

Leavened bread dough
2 tablespoons lard
1 teaspoon lemon juice
1 onion, chopped
2 pounds white broccoli
Sea salt
Pepper
1 clove garlic, finely chopped
10 ounces (1 1/4 cups) ground pork
10 ounces (1 1/4 cups) diced pork
1 tablespoon *strattu* (tomato extract) diluted with 1 glass dry white wine
8 ounces (1 cup) fresh ricotta
4 to 6 tablespoons freshly grated pecorino

Tomato sauce

Extra-virgin olive oil
1 clove garlic, chopped
1 tomato, peeled, seeded, and chopped
Fresh basil leaves

Take the dough and knead in a few of tablespoons of lard and some lemon juice. Cut from this 2 round pieces, one large enough to cover the bottom and sides of a large round baking dish, and a smaller one to place on top of the pie.

Brown half the chopped onion in olive oil in a heavy-bottomed casserole. Parboil the broccoli, drain, and chop into medium-sized pieces. Then toss these into the heavy-bottomed casserole. Mix with the onion and season with salt and pepper.

Prepare a tomato sauce. Coat the bottom of a skillet with olive oil, add the garlic, remaining onion, and tomato. Simmer until it becomes thick, then toss in torn basil leaves.

Fry a finely chopped garlic clove in a large skillet and add the ground pork and diced pork. After a few minutes, add a tablespoon of tomato extract. Once this has almost evaporated, add 1 cup of the tomato sauce and continue simmering for 1 hour, making sure to add water if the mixture becomes too dry. Pour this *ragù* into a large mixing bowl with the broccoli, ricotta, and pecorino, and combine thoroughly. Pour the finished mixture into the prepared pie dish, place the second circle of dough on top and seal the edges. Bake in a preheated 350° oven until golden.

VEGETABLE PIES
Cudduruni

This is a pie recipe very popular throughout the Siracusa area.

Ingredients

Leavened bread dough (or short-crust pastry)
1 large onion, finely sliced
1 cauliflower, about 2 pounds
Several anchovies, chopped
Several pitted black olives, chopped
Pecorino or *caciocavallo* cheese
Extra-virgin olive oil
Pepper
1 egg, beaten or milk for sealing pastry

Tomato sauce

Extra-virgin olive oil
1 clove garlic, crushed and chopped
1 tomato, peeled, seeded, and chopped
Fresh basil leaves

Roll out the dough or pastry and cut it into 4-inch circles.

Prepare a simple tomato sauce. Coat the bottom of a skillet with olive oil and add the crushed garlic and tomato. Simmer until the sauce thickens, then toss in torn basil leaves.

Coat the bottom of a skillet with olive oil and fry the onion. Meanwhile, boil the cauliflower in a large pot of salted water until cooked through, then drain and slice it.

In a large mixing bowl, combine the tomato sauce, onion, and cauliflower along with anchovies to taste, olives, cheese, and olive oil, mixing well. Season with pepper.

Place a few tablespoons of this filling on half of each circle and fold over, pinching the edges together well, and sealing with egg or milk so that the filling does not escape during baking.

Bake the pies in a preheated 400° oven on well-greased baking sheets until golden.

sausage pies
'Nfigghiulata

This "pie" originated in Rosolini, but is found everywhere in the Province of Siracusa. 'Nfigghiulata is a dialect word meaning to "make a strange mixture," or "mix unlike ingredients," or "kind of pie with diverse ingredients." A more prosaic name, and one that is backed up by the technique used in its preparation, would be l'ingravidata — Pregnant Pie. The more sausage and cheese used in the filling, the better the pies will be.

Ingredients
>Leavened bread dough or short crust pastry
>Extra-virgin olive oil
>Tomato sauce (see previous recipe)
>Fresh ricotta
>1 onion, finely chopped
>Wild fennel or baby fennel leaves, chopped
>Fresh or dried pork sausage, crumbled into pieces

Roll out the dough about 1/2 inch thick and cut out 7-inch circles. Brush olive oil over each circle and cover with tomato sauce, ricotta, onion, fennel and broken-up sausage. Now begins the procedure called *aggnutticari*, a dialect word referring to the method of folding the pastry, which is the defining characteristic of this dish. Fold one outside quarter of the circle over the center and repeat with the opposite side, oiling the upper surfaces. Fold each side over the center so that the filling is encased with 4 layers of pastry, now rectangular in shape. Seal the outside edges. Place these on a greased baking sheet and bake in a preheated 400° oven for 20 minutes.

Variations
The variations are minor, including the addition of garlic, parsley, or chili.

Pizza Scacciùni

A type of pizza typical of Carlentini. Roll out a circle of pizza dough until quite thin. Create a raised border and fill the pizza with tomato sauce or finely-chopped very mature tomato pulp, *caciocavallo*, oregano leaves, chopped black pitted olives, chopped anchovy fillets, and salt. Drizzle with plenty of olive oil and bake.

EELS
Anciddi e Capitùna

Although it is traditional all over Italy to prepare eels on Christmas Eve, the residents of Siracusa do not wait until that occasion as eels are always available at the local fish market. The following is one of many ways of preparing eels. In my opinion, it is the best.

Ingredients
- Eels, 1 per serving
- 1 garlic clove, chopped, per eel
- Extra-virgin olive oil
- 1 medium tomato per eel, peeled, seeded, and chopped
- Fresh flat-leaf parsley, chopped
- Pepper
- Several tablespoons white wine
- Bay leaves
- Sea salt

Slice the eels into medium lengths. In a large saucepan, gently fry the garlic in plenty of olive oil until transparent, then add the tomato, parsley, pepper, and white wine. Cook for 5 minutes after it comes to a boil. Salt to taste and add another drizzle of fresh olive oil, then add the eels. Bring this to a boil and cook for another 15 to 20 minutes (it should be very dense).

Create a layer of bay leaves on a serving dish and arrange the eels on top of them, finishing with the sauce.

Capitùna are large eels. Eels are mysterious animals whose vital cycle is little understood. They are abundant in Sicily and Sicilians have eaten them through the centuries, disregarding the injunction against their consumption by both the Islamic and Jewish religions (for hygienic-sanitary reasons more than for religious concerns).

"drunken" snails

Scaùzzi o 'Ntuppattieddi 'mbriachi

This very simple recipe is the most common one used in homes. It is also a traditional dish on the Feast of the Ascension in Floridia.

Ingredients
  4 pounds snails
  1 glass extra-virgin olive oil
  4 to 6 cloves garlic, chopped
  Peperoncino, hot red chili pepper, sliced [or dried flakes] to taste
  1 spring onion, chopped
  1 glass dry white wine
  Sea salt

Purge, rinse, and drain the snails.

In a large saucepan with a lid, add the olive oil, garlic, chili, and spring onion and turn up the heat.

Once the pan is quite hot, add the snails and combine thoroughly, pouring in a glass of white wine. Cover and lower the heat, allowing the snails to cook through for at least 30 minutes.

Façade of Siracusa's cathedral, built around the ancient Greek Temple of Athena

Artichokes with Saint Bernard Sauce
Cacuocciuli câ sarsa San Birnardu

I have already had something to say about various sauces thus far, and the sarsa di San Birnardu *is worth mentioning. With it origins in antiquity (it can be traced back to 1600), this sauce was served at the tables of barons. Some claim it originated in western Sicily, others claim it was at Catania in the Convent of Saint Bernard referred to in Federico De Roberto's* I Vicerè (The Viceroys). *In any case, the nobles mixed socially and it is likely that when exchanging the most refined recipes, this was passed around with a few subtle variations either from west to east or from east to west.*

This sauce is ideal with artichokes, but can be used with any other relatively bland vegetable such as broccoli and cauliflower and even on boiled meat.

Ingredients (for the sauce)
    4 or 5 salted anchovies, scaled and deboned
    6 ounces (3/4 cup) toasted almonds, pounded
    1/3 cup sugar
    2 tablespoons dark bitter chocolate
    1/3 cup crustless, soft bread, torn into pieces
    1 tablespoon extra-virgin olive oil

    Artichokes

Pound the anchovies with a mortar and pestle. Place the pounded anchovies in a mixing bowl and combine with all the other ingredients except the olive oil. Whisk the oil in gradually in a thin stream until the sauce emulsifies to a smooth, creamy consistency.

Meanwhile, boil the artichokes until soft in a large pot, remove any tough outer leaves [and the stems and "chokes"], and spoon the sauce into the hearts and serve.

The Saint Bernard in question is the one born in 1091 who founded the Monastery of Clairvaux. In one of his letters to his nephew Robert, he used a Latin phrase that still rings true, *satis est ad omne condimentum sal cum fame*, "whenever hunger is present, the only condiment you need is salt," meaning that when you are hungry everything tastes good. While the apostolic reference embedded in the quotation is clear, it is not clear why this extremely rich sauce, with expensive ingredients and a sophisticated method of preparation, quite contrary to any monkish principle of temperance regarding the stomach, should be associated with the Saint. But that is just another riddle of society.

STUFFED ARTICHOKES
Cacuocciuli fritti a cirvieddu

There are millions of different ways to prepare artichokes. Everywhere they are cooked on the grill or fried in a pan. They are stuffed with mixtures of garlic, parsley, chopped anchovies, bread crumbs, salt, and olive oil that are forced among the leaves.

The following recipe is a classic, meaning "artichokes in the style of brains," that was always included in important meals as part of a fritto misto (mixed fry). Meat in the form of a cutlet was served together with brains, artichokes, meatballs, and halved hard-boiled eggs that were breaded and fried.

Ingredients
> Artichokes
> Flour
> 1 beaten egg
> Bread crumbs
> Extra-virgin olive oil
> Sea salt

Set out plates of flour and bread crumbs for dredging.

Remove the tougher leaves of the artichokes and leave about 1 inch of stem, then boil them in a saucepan. Drain well and dry, then quarter each [removing any "chokes"]. Dip the segments first in flour, then in the egg, and finally in the bread crumbs to coat.

In a heavy-bottomed casserole, deep-fry the artichoke quarters in a generous amount of very hot olive oil until golden. Sprinkle with salt and serve hot.

Artichokes have different names that vary from area to area. They all derive from the Arabic root *al-kharshuf*, which also gave us the Italian name, *carciofo*. It was known to Romans with the name of *cynara* but for unknown reasons its cultivation waned. Its cultivation resumed after the arrival of the Arabs in Sicily (around 900) and then during the Middle Ages when they were imported from Ethiopia and became common in Tuscany and the Veneto region. Their production became more intense in Sicily during the 16th century.

Cutuletti di milinciani

THE same procedure to prepare meat cutlets for a fritto misto can be used with thick slices of eggplant with skins on. They are dipped in flour, and egg, and then fried and served with a sprinkle of salt.

EGGPLANT "BOATS"
Milinciani a varcuzza

Ingredients
- 1 eggplant per serving
- Sea salt
- 1 ripe tomato per serving, peeled and seeded, and roughly chopped
- Extra-virgin olive oil
- Sugar
- White wine vinegar
- Cinnamon
- Almonds, toasted and crushed

The refined chef will call these "little boats" of eggplant. Slice the whole eggplants into large wedges (hence the "boat" shape) that are then salted and left to sweat. Rinse and pat dry. Coat the bottom of a heavy pot with olive oil and fry wedges until golden on the outside (do not worry if they are not cooked through).

In a separate saucepan, briefly cook the tomatoes in olive oil with salt and a pinch of sugar for each tomato.

Arrange the eggplants in a heavy-bottomed casserole, cover with the tomato mixture, and a sprinkle of sugar and wine vinegar. Cover and cook until the sauce has thickened. Transfer eggplants and sauce to a serving platter, and dust with cinnamon and crushed almonds.

cheese

ALTHOUGH not a large variety of cheeses are produced around Siracusa, the quality of those that are is exceptional. Pecorino, particularly the one from Sortino, is very good and the local *caciocavallo* competes on equal footing with the one made in Ragusa. There is widespread production of ricotta, which is usually eaten fresh, but the salted and baked versions are noteworthy.

Baked ricotta Ricotta 'nfurnata

It is a classic tradition in the area around Siracusa to take salted ricotta and bake it in a very hot oven until it acquires the characteristic bronze color. The cheese thus obtained is incorporated in recipes in a variety of different ways, usually grated over pasta with tomato-based sauces or baked pasta. It can also be used as a substitute for pecorino in stuffing and eaten alone with bread.

A field of prickly pears

fruits

siracusa is also an abundant producer of fruit. One of the more recently introduced citrus varieties is a green-skinned lemon that is the largest source of wealth in the agricultural economy. Almonds are next in importance—especially the variety from Avola known as *pizzuta* that has earned the E.U. stamp.* The traditional sugar coated candies known as *confetti* are made from these almonds, and prized for their perfect oval shape.

Fruit of every kind is cultivated in Siracusa. Notable among these are the medlar fruits of Noto, strawberries from Avola (once sold in traditional little woven cane baskets), a thick skinned lemon known as *piretto*, also from Noto, and table grapes from Pachino.

There is not a single community in the area that does not grow quinces from which the splendid *cutugnata,* quince jelly, is made.

sweets
Baked Goods, Desserts, and Confectionary

THE region abounds in a wide variety of sweets that come into their full glory during Christmas, Easter, and the Feast Days of various patron saints.

*The European Union Protected Denomination of Origin stamp identifies a unique and significant product in a specific region or town. Its geographical origin determines its quality or particular characteristics. Production of the product may only be carried out in its specified area.

Almonds start flowering in Sicily during the month of January. It is the first flowering that nature provides us. They are cultivated everywhere on the island, but the areas around Agrigento and Siracusa seem the most suited to them. The prestigious "Festival of the Flowering Almonds" takes place in Agrigento. This very pleasing dried fruit has been used widely: to make typical sweets like nougats; as flour which when combined with sugar make the famous Martorana fruits; and to make drinks like almond milk, or puddings (blanc mange). But that's not all. Almonds are used even today in "salted" cooking mixed with meat (such as the exceptional meatballs with toasted almonds), with fish in certain typical recipes, and even with vegetables.

RICOTTA TARTS
Cassateddi

The following recipe is the traditional one that originated at Ferla but is now widely used in the entire region, even crossing over into the Ragusa area.

Ingredients

For the pastry sheets
6 cups flour
3/4 cup sugar
1/2 cup lard

For the ricotta filling
3 cups fresh ricotta
1 cup sugar
2 eggs, beaten
Cinnamon

Make a pastry with the flour, sugar, and lard, and knead thoroughly. On a smooth work surface, roll it out into thin sheets and cut out 4-inch circles. Then cut small strips with the leftover pastry.

Combine the ricotta, sugar, eggs, and a pinch of cinnamon in a mixing bowl. Spread this mixture about 1/2 inch deep in the center of each pastry circle, then crimp the edges all around to create small tarts. Place 2 small strips of pastry in the form of a cross on the centers of each. Bake on non-stick sheets in a preheated 350° oven until the tarts are golden.

Various similar tarts known in dialect as *cassate, cassatelle,* and *cassatine* are associated with Easter because once they were prepared only on this holiday.

rice fritters
Crispeddi di risu

These fritters are prepared all over Sicily and are traditional at the Feast of St. Joseph. They exist in various forms, differing in ingredients and preparation techniques, and appreciated everywhere. This is a recipe typical of Siracusa.

Ingredients
  2 1/2 cups cooked rice, cooled
  Zest of 2 lemons
  4 cups flour
  2 ounces brewers' yeast, dissolved in lukewarm water
  Extra-virgin olive oil
  Honey, melted

In a large mixing bowl, combine cooled rice, lemon zest, flour, and yeast. Stir the mixture until it becomes firm, but not hard. Set aside to rise for 1 hour.

Drop tablespoons of the batter into a heavy-bottomed pot filled with boiling oil. Fry the fritters in batches until golden brown. Drain and serve, drizzled with hot melted honey.

BOILED WHEAT AND RICOTTA PUDDING
Cuccìa

I find it irritating that this most satisfying dessert, which requires only the most basic amount of preparation, is made only on Feast Days and not throughout the year. Even more irritating is that no restaurants—which are usually only too eager to steal other people's recipes and ideas—have bothered to offer cuccìa, *not even for the Feast of St. Lucy.*

Ingredients

    4 cups wheat, in whole grains, cleaned, rinsed, soaked overnight, and dried
    1 1/2 cups fresh ricotta
    1 3/4 cups sugar
    1/2 cup assorted candied fruit, chopped
    Shaved chocolate
    Cinnamon

Boil the whole wheat grains in fresh water until tender. They must not be underdone or overcooked. Drain after cooking and set aside to cool.

Meanwhile, combine the ricotta and sugar with a whisk (add a little milk if the mixture is too dry) until a homogenous cream forms. Stir in a handful of shaved chocolate, candied fruit, and a pinch of cinnamon. Mound the boiled wheat on a serving dish and cover with the ricotta mixture. Decorate with more candied fruit and serve.

QUINCE JELLIES
Cutugnata

As we know, quinces are inedible raw. The only way to enjoy quince is to make a conserve, which is prepared so that once dried it can be eaten like a candy. It was once served to children as a snack or at Sunday lunch. Although found all over Sicily, the best come from Noto and Palazzolo Acreide.

Ingredients
- 2 pounds quinces
- Sugar
- 3 lemons
- Laurel leaves

Boil the washed quinces in water with the lemons for 30 minutes, then remove the lemons, drain and set quinces aside to cool. Once cooled, peel, core, and press through a fine sieve. Put the cold quince purée into a saucepan and combine with an equal amount of sugar. Bring to a boil, stirring continuously so it doesn't stick to the bottom of the pan. Once the mixture begins to bubble, lower the heat and simmer, still stirring, until this becomes homogenous and topaz in color. Be sure not to overcook or it will turn dark.

Spoon the mixture into small molds and leave them in the sun for several days to dry (bringing them in overnight to avoid moisture).

Drying time will depend on how hot the days are and can vary from 2 to 4 days or more. Take them out of their molds, turn them over, and leave out again for several more days to continue drying on the other side.

Once they are dry on both sides (but still moist in the center), they are traditionally stored on a bed of laurel leaves in tin containers with tight-fitting lids.

The most common use for quince is the *cutugnata*, although in Nicosia they make a *cudugnata* that prescribes cooking the peeled quinces in cooked wine must and serving them as dessert. The Salerno School of Medicine declared openly that "When eaten raw, the anus will trumpet, but represents food and medicine." The symbolism associated with quinces became emblematic of sadness, bitterness, and affliction, so much so that in Sicilian, and in Italian as well, *inghiottir cotogne* (to swallow quinces) means "receiving insults without the ability to react in kind" and *cotogne di fidanzati* (lovers's quarrels).

ST. CLAIRE'S BIG FACE
Facciùni di Santa Chiara

Do not be deceived by the name, as there is no blasphemy intended. This is actually a cake traditionally prepared by the nuns of the Convent of St. Claire at Noto who used to decorate the top of the cake with a large ruddy angel's face with silver wings sprouting from behind made from colored paper. The reason for this may be either the nuns' devotion to the Guardian Angel or the fact that other types of decoration might have been beyond their budget!

Ingredients
    Almond paste
    Lime marmelade
    Large round sponge cake, sliced in half horizontally
    Orange marmelade
    Chocolate frosting, enough to cover the cake
    Sugar sprinkles

Take a baker's round cardboard cake base and spread over it a thin layer of softened almond paste. Over this, spread lime marmelade and top with one of the sponge cake rounds.

Turn this over and remove the cardboard leaving the marzipan layer face up. Spread this with orange marmelade and place the second cake round on top. Ice the top and sides completely with the chocolate frosting and decorate with sprinkles. Decorate with a large homemade paper angel face.

Gnuocculi

This is a specialty from Canicattini Bagni. The simple ingredients contrast with the rather difficult technique for preparing it, especially for the braiding required to shape the sweet.

Ingredients
> 6 cups flour
> 6 eggs
> Extra-virgin olive oil
> Sugar
> Cinnamon

Make a dough with the flour and eggs, kneading well and rolling out in very thin sheets, "as thin as the host." Cut strips 1 inch by 5 or 6 inches long. Braid the strips like locks of hair and pile one set of braids on another, delicately. Then shape them into the form of doughnuts. Bring a generous amount of olive oil to a boil in a heavy-bottomed pot and fry the fritters until they are golden. Remove gently and drain on paper towels. Sprinkle with sugar and cinnamon.

Meringues
Miringhi o Scumi o Scumini o Scumiddi

The different names, derived from the French meringue and the Italian schiuma *or "froth" reflect some local differences, although the basic recipe is the same throughout Sicily.*

Ingredients
> 10 egg whites
> 5 cups sugar
> Vanilla extract

Beat the egg whites and sugar, flavored with a few drops of vanilla, until they form a stiff froth. Drop spoonfuls of the mixture onto a greased baking sheet and bake in a preheated 350° oven until they begin to look golden.

Variations
Variations include reducing the amount of sugar to 1 1/4 cups, adding ground toasted almonds, or decorating them prior to baking with candy sprinkles.

FrIeD Pasta sIracusa- style
Pasta fritta a sirausana

A specialty of Siracusa unique in Sicily and probably descended from sussameli, *a curiosity that needs to be revived in every home.*

Ingredients
    Very fine pasta such as *capelli d'angelo* (angel-hair pasta)
    Lard
    Honey
    Cinnamon (optional)

Bring a large pot of salted water to a boil and cook some *capelli d'angelo* until al dente.

Drain, then take small quantities, twist with a fork into small skeins and drop them into boiling lard in a heavy-bottomed pot. As soon as they harden and become golden, remove gently and drain on paper towels. Move them to a serving platter and drizzle with abundant melted honey. They can also be dusted with cinnamon.

People take the origin of the term *sussameli* from a combination of *sesamo* (sesame) and *meli* (honey) because the creation was garnished with honey and could have been covered with sesame seed. Another possible origin could have been suggested by the fact that the preparation requires a lot of honey which is "sucked up," that is, absorbed by the flour. Both obviously are conjectures. The correct origin of the term derives from the fact that *sussameli* means "honeysucker" and refers to a type of dried pasta, like small *maccarruna*, which was given this name because of the function assigned to it. Many centuries ago, when pasta was born, people sought to dress it in many ways. During holidays it was dressed with melted honey, and children and adults alike sucked the honey, more or less noisily, as they ate it.

Rice with Honey
Risu ccô meli

That rice pilaf is a recipe of Indian origin goes without saying, but how is it that here we have an ancient recipe that seems to be a direct descendant? Some mysteries regarding things culinary cannot be explained.

Ingredients
> 1 1/2 cups (3 sticks) butter
> 1 1/4 cups honey
> 2 1/2 cups uncooked rice
> 8 tablespoons (1/2 cup) raisins
> Cinnamon

In a saucepan, melt the butter with the honey, then pour the mixture into a baking dish. Stir in the rice and combine, then bake in a preheated 350° oven for 20 to 25 minutes. Remove the dish from the oven, add 1 quart of water and the raisins. Stir to combine thoroughly, and return to the oven. Check from time to time to make sure that the rice has not absorbed all the water while cooking and add a little boiling water if it prematurely dries out. The rice must end up fluffy and tender and quite dry.

Serve cold, sprinkled with cinnamon.

nouGaT Meringue
Scuma di turruni

This recipe was obviously invented by senior citizens who had no teeth left but who still wanted to taste turruni!

Ingredients
> Raw almonds, peeled and chopped
> Sugar
> 6 egg whites

Measure the ingredients so that for each ounce of chopped almonds an equal measure of sugar is used. Combine these in a saucepan over medium heat until the sugar has caramelized. Spread the *turruni* (*torrone* in Italian) mixture on a cold baking sheet and allow to cool. Once it is cold and hard, smash it into small pieces, then continue with a mortar and pestle until it is in fine grains. Beat the egg whites until they form stiff peaks then stir in the "crumbs." Pour the mixture into a mold and cook it in a bain-marie until the egg whites set.

saInT LuCY's specTacLes
Ucciali di Santa Lucia

The recipe for this traditional fritter prepared during the grape harvest is named after Saint Lucy, the Patron Saint of Siracusa, who is venerated throughout Sicily as the protector of sight and for her martyrdom.

Ingredients
> 6 cups flour
> 2 eggs
> *Mosto*, grape must (see page 194)
> Almonds, toasted and ground

On a smooth work surface, make a dough with the flour and eggs as if for pasta. Divide and roll the dough into long thin sausage shapes similar to *grissini*. Cut these into lengths of a few inches, giving the ends a twist to resemble the shape of spectacles. Gently drop them individually into a heavy-bottomed pot of simmering grape must and allow them to boil gently for about 30 minutes. Drain and serve, sprinkled with almonds.

almond cake
Torta di mennuli

Many types of almond cake are found throughout Sicily's provinces with various ingredients.
They are particularly prominent in Siracusa and Agrigento (the main producers of almonds)
and Palermo (the "gluttonous" province). This is the version in Siracusa.

Ingredients
15 eggs, separated
2 1/2 cups sugar
Vanilla extract, several drops
Zest of 1 lemon
Small glass of sweet liqueur
1 pound toasted almonds, ground coarsely

In a large mixing bowl, beat the egg whites until they are stiff. In another bowl, beat together the sugar and egg yolks with the vanilla, lemon zest, and a sweet liqueur. Once this mixture is well beaten, blend in the toasted almonds and gently fold in the beaten egg whites. Combine, taking care to keep the mixture as fluffy as possible.

Pour into greased and floured cake pans and bake in a preheated 350° oven until golden.

wines

THere are two *Denominazione di Origine Controllata (DOC)* wines, or Wines of Designated Origin, in the area around Siracusa—the *Moscato di Noto* and the *Moscato di Siracusa,* both muscatel wines.

At Pachino, the once ancient winemaking center famous for its past tradition of producing fine table wines, there is no longer a single cellar bottling wine. Only at Rosolini is there a single Cantina Sociale, or wine co-operative, producing *Eloro* red, white, and rosé wines.

But in the context of Sicilian wine production, this area, including the southeastern part of the island, is of great prominence. The vineyards growing white wine grapes produce wines characterized by their delicacy and a certain degree of pleasant acidity touched with fruit flavors, bordering in some cases on the tropical. Among the white wine varieties are *Cataratto, Albanello, Damaschino Grecanico,* and *Chardonnay.*

This is also a very important area for the production of red wines. Vineyards producing specialized red wine grapes are widespread. The most outstanding among them is the *Nero d'Avola* or *Calabrese,* which is considered indigenous to the area around Siracusa. These wines are renowned for body, elegance, and structure.

The Italian government has identified and awarded the DOC to unique and significant wines in specific regions or towns. Their geographical origin determines quality and particular characteristics.

liqueurs

In this area, there is no commercial production of distilled liquor. To compensate, some families make a homemade liqueur, *rosoliu*, with lemon, following to this day an ancient recipe.

Rosoliu di lumia (Lemon Liqueur)

One of the oldest recipes for homemade liqueur, it can be also be flavored with mandarins, oranges, or limes.

Ingredients

Zest of 5 fresh almost-ripe lemons
8 ounces (1 cup) alcohol [pure, distilled]
5 cups sugar
1 quart water
16 ounces (2 cups) alcohol [pure, distilled]

Zest the rind of the lemons that have been picked before they are fully mature (the skin should still be greenish), taking care to not grate the white pith. Immerse the rind in 8 ounces of alcohol and let steep for a week. Dissolve 5 cups of sugar in 1 quart of water and boil only for a few minutes. Allow to cool, then add to the alcohol in lemon rind with another 16 ounces of alcohol. Set aside for 2 to 3 days, then filter and pour into clean, dry bottles and tightly seal. It is a good rule to allow the bottles to sit for at least a month in order to stabilize.

Variations
The quantities of alcohol and sugar can be adjusted according to personal preference.

ragusa and its province

THere are two principal reasons why the cooking of Ragusa in unknown to many. First, this southernmost province in Sicily—its latitude is lower than that of Tunisia—is an area that has tended to be cut off from the typical tourist circuit, in spite of the fact that it is rich in natural beauty. Here we find centuries-old carob trees, the last oasis for the species in Europe;[1] fifty-six miles of coastline and pristine seas; architectural ruins such as the ancient city of Kamarina;[2] the remains of the ancient cave dwellings of the Cava d'Ispica; the *Fonte di Diana*, Fountain of Diana;[3] and noteworthy architecture, including the one hundred Baroque churches scattered throughout twelve municipalities. Rich in local folklore and enjoying a wealth of local traditions, Ragusa is an important center of culture and has contributed many illustrious men in all cultural disciplines.

Second. The local restaurant industry rarely offers those few tourists who find themselves in the area any of the local traditional dishes, as if they were ashamed of their humble culinary origins and recoil from revealing them.

The true cooking of Ragusa is found among local families who still prepare most of their complex traditional dishes. Given the times, as women are increasingly staying away from the kitchen, I do not know how much longer this culinary oasis can survive.

The Ragusans are great eaters of pasta. In fact, first courses have over time become ever more sumptuous: baked pasta, little semolina gnocchi, lasagne, and ravioli with a variety of sauces, plus the beloved *ragù,* are the favorites. Some of the peasant dishes that had humble beginnings, for example *bruoru di maiali*, pork broth, gradually became absorbed into the cooking of the wealthy, *cucina ricca.*

While fish is widely eaten, fish specialties are relatively few in number. Yet along the very long coastline from Pozzallo to Scoglitti, small private boats, as well as the fleets from Pozzallo and Donnalucata, bring in their catch fresh every day. It is one of the few coastlines where sea urchins[4] and cockles still reign among the rocks and sand.

1. A great, majestic, and exceptional tree that lives in the Iblei Mountains (see page 160). In ancient times, carobs broken into pieces were used as additives to animal food and also to extract sugar and alcohol. Human consumption was limited, although carobs are tasty when baked in the oven. Together with toasted

A Baroque church in the city of Ragusa

chickpeas and *mostarda e cotognata*, carobs were part of a peasant cuisine offered on special occasions such as baptisms, christenings, and even weddings. The seeds have long been used in making ice cream (it makes the ice cream soft). Currently, studies are being conducted on the use of carob flour to make sweets and to use as an additive in dieting.

2. The city of Kamarina, whose ruins are still openly visible, was founded by the Greeks and rose to become a great power. There was a smelly swamp near the city that the inhabitants wanted to drain, but before doing so they consulted Apollo's oracle. Unfortunately, the response was *Kamarinam ne moveas,* meaning "Kamarina must not move." Nevertheless, considering that the smelly swamp was a cause of disease, they decided to ignore the god's will. The city was then attacked by its enemies, who gained easy access across the drained part of the swamp that no longer protected it. Ancient writers attributed Kamarina's fall to its' citizens disdain for the oracle.

3. This is a fountain in the town-hall square of Comiso, which was founded by the Greeks. The 16th-century historian Tomasso Fazello recalled

On the other hand, typical meat dishes, unlike elsewhere in Sicily, figure heavily among traditional fare, especially pork. Ragusa favors pork,[5] with beef and poultry coming close behind. Some traditional dishes have gained ascendancy over time. Veritable classics include whole stuffed chicken; rabbit stew; stuffed cutlets; tripe Ragusa-style; baked or glazed lamb, and lamb baked in bread crust. (Horsemeat is excluded from the table everywhere.)[6]

The rustic oven offers great variety, including *scacce* and *'mpanate*.[7] On the plains around Vittoria, there is intense agricultural cultivation in enormous complexes of greenhouses as well as on acres of open fields, resulting in innumerable dishes with fresh ingredients including tomatoes, eggplants, artichokes, peppers, zucchini—to be eaten either raw or cooked. On the plains we find the ever-present sun-dried tomato, or *capuliatu*, (see page 83) and above all *strattu*, sun-dried tomato extract formed into balls and preserved. It takes twenty-two pounds of fresh tomatoes to make just two pounds of *strattu*.

Legumes deserve special mention. There is another staple typical of the higher zones of the Iblei Mountains of Ragusa and Modica. I am referring especially to fava beans, a magic food that continues its tradition here in the famous *maccu* that once was nearly the daily staple for peasant families. I am also referring to the *ciciruocculu*, or *cicerchia*,[8] which still survives in Monterosso, where it is dried and ground into flour for rustic mixtures; and to a variety of wild herbs with very strange names that gourmets favor greatly, paying handsomely for them to the street vendors who set up shop at strategic corners of the cities.

At Chiaramonte Gulfi and Frigintini, one of the most flavorsome and aromatic olive oils on the island is produced, the use of which certainly contributes to the success of their recipes. Ispica produces

that the water of this fountain could not be mixed with wine if the person trying to do so was unchaste or sullied. Husbands who were suspicious of their wives' fidelity brought them to the fountain to make certain that they were faithful. The 17th-century historian Antonino Mongitore made the following remark regarding Fazello's report: ". . . it is more likely that the devil had a hand in it, in as much as this artifice allowed a number of wife-killings."

4. The females are laden with eggs during the full moon, according to popular belief. In Sicilian they are known as *rizzi*, but also as *marancituli*. This odd name is derived from two different terms: the Latin *ericius* that means earth urchin, and its diminutive *ericitulus*, meaning small earth urchin. These evolved first into *ancitula* and then, by analogy, into *marancitula*, sea urchin.

5. In addition to being accused of greed and lust, the pig was also deemed to be acquisitive. In this regard, St. Bernard (see page 138) remarked that "the acquisitive man is like the pig: he makes people happy only on the day of his death." A Sicilian saying characterizes the

pig as a bearer of joy: "If you want to be happy for one day, shave; if you want to be happy for a month, get married; and if you want to be happy for a year, slaughter a pig." In reality, the killing of pigs for food that would last a long time was a common practice in the countryside and in the city. The ideal time for this was just before Christmas. In Sicily, despite an Arab invasion, there was no Islamic prohibition against the consumption of pork. Nevertheless, the fact remains that until the 1950s, for hygienic and sanitary reasons—before refrigerators were widely available—the slaughter of the first pig had to be sanctioned by the Prefect and could not occur before the feast of Saint Martin. The last pig had to be slaughtered before Easter.

6. Sicilians find eating horsemeat instinctively repulsive and unnatural. There is a simple reason for this: donkeys, horses, and mules were "house animals," not only because they are silent helpers in man's daily toil, but because they are seen as companions in long and lonely cart journeys, as well as sentinels during restless nights spent out in the deserted fields. How could anyone eat this meat?

7. These are characteristic *rosticceria*, still quite common in homes, bakeries, and specialized stores. They are classic *focacce:* the *scacce* are generally rectangular in shape (a sheet of dough folded like a book) always stuffed with vegetables; *'mpanate* are round and thicker. Their stuffing can be made with vegetables, but can include meat and fish. Both *scacce* and *'mpanate* are baked in

the oven, producing their golden crust.

8. A legume similar to the pea. The plant produces seeds that resemble the chickpea, but they are not spherical in shape and they have asymmetric spurs resembling stars. Its use has always been limited: in Monterosso they were used to make a flour to cook in a polenta.

9. It owes its name to the Greek words *glikis* (sweet) and *riza* (root). In Sicilian it is often called *rigulizia*, which clearly displays its etymological roots. It is very rich in estrogens and female hormones, as science has recently shown, but this fact is not widely known among its consumers. Perhaps for this reason, according to popular belief, chewing licorice roots makes a woman passionately sensual.

Carob trees near Modica

wonderful carrots due to the unique composition of its soil. At Giarratana, a variety of white onion is grown known as the *bianca di Giarratana* that has earned the European Union Protected Denomination of Origin stamp (see page 143) for its large size and non-pungent sweetness. The very best wild thyme called *satra* grows in Santa Croce Camerina. In the shade of the centuries-old majestic carob trees, oregano grows wild on the Iblei Mountains. Acate provides splendid table grapes and gigantic artichokes. In the surrounding countryside, if one looks for them carefully in the fields, wild liquorice roots[9] can be found. Every corner of Ragusa seems to have its own culinary story to tell.

Due to the richness of the highland soil, the clement climate, and the experience of herdsmen, cheeses and other milk products are deservedly famous. Ragusan *caciocavallo*, richly flavored, is sold in rectangular blocks instead of the round shape found in other Sicilian areas, and is marketed under the name *ragusano* to distinguish it.

Desserts and confections in the Ragusa province are quite difficult to find and not widely-known outside the area, but fortunately certain ancient traditional recipes continue to be made and sold by numerous pastry shops—so they will certainly endure. The most typical are included here and follow the original recipes.

PORK BROTH
Bruoru di maiali

Don't let the name fool you! This is a "dry" first course dish, belonging to cucina baronale that became popular during the Baroque era. Despite its name, this recipe is actually not a broth, but a dish that has survived from the noble tables of the Baroque era. It is actually only a variation of gelatina di maiale, or pork gelatin, and is a dish that makes use of those parts of the animal that are not for sale as meat—the bones, cartilage and so on. A monsu [a chef of a noble household hired from France] not satisfied with the humble origins of this dish, went on to make an elaborate affair of it, adding expensive ingredients in order to sufficiently elevate it to a status suitable for the baronial table. The following recipe was recently rediscovered in an old family recipe book and is published here for the first time.

Ingredients

To be prepared	For the broth
Minced pork	Proportionately, 2 parts pork bones
Red wine	(shoulder and spine), 1 part veal knuckles
Pepper	Water
Sea salt	Sprig of wild thyme (*satra*)
1 tablespoon *caciocavallo ragusano*, grated	Saffron
1 onion, thinly sliced	Cinnamon
Lard	1 teaspoon pepper
Maccheroncini [small ziti]	Sea salt

The night before serving, for each quart of broth to be made mix together: 3 1/2 ounces (1/3 cup) of minced pork, red wine, pepper, salt and 1 tablespoon of *caciocavallo*. Fry the onion in lard until golden. Add the ground pork mixture, and, cooking over low heat, add a little more red wine. When the mixture has finished cooking, set aside to cool.

The next day, in a large stockpot, cook the bones of the pork and the veal in water high enough to cover them, adding a sprig of thyme for every 2 quarts of water, a pinch of saffron and cinnamon, pepper, and salt. Simmer for 2 hours, then filter this and allow the broth to cool. When cooled, degrease it.

Bring the broth back to a boil and add the *maccheroncini*. Once cooked al dente, add the reserved pork mixture, keeping in mind that the dish's consistency should not be overly liquid, but rather thick, and serve. (The original recipe called for homemade *maccheroncini* made in the style of Piazza Armerina: small squares of pasta folded at an angle.)

LITTLE GNOCCHI WITH RAGÙ OR FALSE RAGÙ
Gnucchitti o sucu o sucu fintu

In Sicily, when one says sarsa *(tomato sauce), only plain tomato sauce is indicated.* Sucu *contains a larger quantity of tomatoes, so that it is much thicker and is closer to a* ragù, *or sauce containing meat, even though no meat is actually present—which is why it is also referred to in some areas as* sucu fintu *(false* ragù*).*

This sauce is prepared with tomatoes and the addition of capuliatu *(extremely dense tomato concentrate) and red wine. The mixture is cooked for a long period, allowing it to thicken considerably.*

Ingredients
　2 tablespoons extra-virgin olive oil
　1 tablespoon very finely chopped onion
　1 tablespoon *capuliatu*, tomato concentrate, diluted with 1 teaspoon red wine
　2 pounds large, ripe tomatoes, peeled, seeded, and chopped
　Fresh basil leaves, chopped for the sauce, plus several whole for servings
　Sea salt
　2 cloves garlic, chopped
　Fresh small gnocchi
　Fresh *caciocavallo ragusano*

In a skillet, fry the onion in olive oil to warm it through. Add a tablespoon of diluted tomato concentrate, tomatoes, basil, salt to taste, and garlic. Bring to a boil. Lower the heat and simmer for 1 hour, adding a little water as necessary, until the sauce is very thick.

Cook the gnocchi, drain, and toss with the sauce. Add a basil leaf to each serving and an abundant grating of *caciocavallo*.

BaKeD MaCaronI
Maccarruna o furnu a muricana

One of the many oven-baked pasta dishes common in Sicily and in the Province of Ragusa as well. This one, however, is local and it represents the prototype for all pasta al forno, *both because of the wealth of ingredients and the complex preparation involved, which suggests that it was a dish made for a feast or for special occasions.*

Ingredients

For the ragù
1 onion, sliced
A few tablespoons extra-virgin olive oil
1 tablespoon *strattu* (tomato extract) diluted with 1 teaspoon red wine
3/4 pound ground pork
3/4 pound ground veal
1/4 pound sausage, broken up
1 tomato, peeled, seeded, and chopped
Glass of water

For the shredded meat sauce
1 pound piece of beef
Extra-virgin olive oil
1 small onion, chopped
2 cloves garlic, chopped
Red wine
Sea salt
Fresh basil leaves, chopped
Fresh flat-leaf parsley, chopped
Fresh rosemary
1 celery heart, finely chopped
1 1/2 cups fresh tomatoes, peeled, seeded, and chopped

To complete
1 zucchini, long, thin shaped, cut into discs
4 hard-boiled eggs
Homemade *maccarruna* (macaroni)
Fresh pecorino, sliced
Fresh *caciocavallo ragusano*

To prepare the *ragù*: in a large skillet, fry the sliced onion in olive oil until golden. Mix in the tomato extract, then add the ground pork, veal, and sausage. Stir well for a few minutes, then add the tomato and a glass of water. Mix and continue simmering for at least 1 hour.

Meanwhile, cook the meat and sauce. In a heavy-bottomed casserole, brown the meat in olive oil on all sides. Then add the onion, garlic, and a few of glasses of red wine. Add the salt, herbs, celery heart, fresh tomatoes, and enough water to cover. Simmer at least 2 hours, until the meat can be easily shredded.

As the sauces are finishing, fry the zucchini discs in a pan. Slice the hard-boiled eggs. Bring a pot of salted water to a boil and cook the pasta until al dente, drain, and transfer to a mixing bowl. Dress the pasta with some of the shredded meat sauce.

To assemble: put a layer of pasta in a large baking dish, add a layer of the meat sauce, a layer of *ragù,* slices of egg, slices of fresh pecorino, and an abundant grating of *caciocavallo.* Continue with more layers. The final pasta layer should be topped with the two cheeses. Bake in the oven for 15 minutes.

Fava Bean soup
Maccu di favi

I do not know if this dish actually had its origins in the Ragusa area or in some other locality of the Iblei Mountains, but it is fact that here it continues to be made in every home. Its name, whose etymology and origins have been the subject of many conjectures, testifies that it is very old. Let's try to unravel the mystery.

The ancient Romans ate puls fabacea, *a flour made from dried fava beans and prepared in a soup. Given that nothing has changed over the centuries, it can be assumed that this* puls *is none other than the* maccu *of today with the addition of olive oil and fennel seeds. Let's not forget that the name of a character from ancient Roman* atellanes *[comedies/farces] was Macchus. He was the distant progenitor of today's Pulcinella. Depicted as a glutton constantly eating, his name became associated with the fondness—the craving—that this food evoked.*

Etymologists suggest four Greek words as possible origins. These words are: makron, *long;* makaria, *a paste made from flour and barley, and a votive offering to the gods;* mageiros, *a kind of ancient pastry-chef working with flour, from the verb* macco, *to mix; and* makar, *blessed or holy food (and the root of the name for the food-offering* makaria *above).*

One thing is certain: fava beans have played both a religious and mysterious role in the ancient world.

Maccu exists also in the regions of the Madonie Mountains and in many mountain communities. In Paternò, and in the Siracusa area, it is a traditional dish for the Feast of St. Joseph, where it was once offered on that day to poor girls and orphans.

Through the centuries, fava beans have had both opponents and supporters. The Egyptians and the Greeks maintained that if you wanted to keep death at bay you had to abstain from eating them (Herotodus).

The Celts held the opposite opinion. In fact, they associated the fava bean with fertility.

Pythagoras hated them, claiming that they "smelled like human seed." Cicero explained this aversion with the fact that they heat the intestines and disturb divining dreams. Ovid related that witches chewed on fava beans while they were concocting their spells designed to paralyze the tongues of their enemies. At one time, fava beans were connected with death in Christian culture.

The connection between fava beans and death originates in Egyptian and Greek thought and it is based on the following: the fava is the only plant with a trunk that has no support, no knots and is hollow inside; its flowers are white, but dotted with black (a symbol of the nether world of the dead that is a very rare occurrence among vegetables). In addition, the black spot reproduces the

Ingredients
  1 pound dried fava beans, peeled and soaked overnight
  Sea salt
  A small bunch of wild fennel or 1 teaspoon fennel seeds
  Extra-virgin olive oil
  Peperoncino, hot red chili pepper, chopped [or dried flakes] to taste
  Small fresh lasagne sheets (optional)

Greek letter for *thànatos*, death. All these factors convinced people that the souls of the dead resided in the fava beans and it was for this reason that in many rituals black fava beans were offered to the infernal divinities.

Rinse the soaked fava beans and place them in a saucepan with enough water to cover and a teaspoon of salt. Bring to a boil, then lower the heat and cook for at least 1 hour, stirring occasionally and breaking up any beans that remain whole.

At this point, add the wild fennel or fennel seeds and continue cooking for another 20 minutes in order to obtain a creamy consistency. Serve the soup drizzled with olive oil and chopped chili.

Alternatively, add extra water to thin the consistency, bring to a boil and add small fresh lasagne sheets [also called *reginette*]. Serve this with olive oil and chili.

Variations

Maccu can be served cold. Once it has cooled, it takes on the consistency of clay and can be cut it into slices, which also can be breaded to fry quickly.

cart Drivers Pasta
Pasta a carrittera

This famous specialty by now well-known in Italy is generally misunderstood by many who prepare it or order it in restaurants. People confuse pasta dressed with fried garlic and olive oil, incorrectly named alla carrettiera *(cart driver-style), which is the one usually served, with the authentic recipe using raw garlic and olive oil.*

It was, in fact, cart drivers—more out of necessity than art—who invented this recipe. As they traveled from town to town, they took along with them in their carretti *(carts) just the basic necessities—long-lasting supplies that needed no special conservation, such as round country bread that lasted a week, salted sardines, garlic, onions, and cheese; and the basics: salt, olive oil, and pasta. They also packed a little terracotta container full of* maccu, *used for the evening meal.*

Ingredients
    1 pound spaghetti
    2 cloves garlic, finely grated
    Peperoncino, hot red chili pepper, chopped [or dried flakes]
    Grated pecorino
    Extra-virgin olive oil

Cook the spaghetti al dente in boiling salted water. Once cooked, drain and toss with garlic, chili to taste, grated pecorino cheese, and olive oil.

Variation
Obviously the garlic can be fried in oil and then used to dress that spaghetti, topped with grated cheese. In this case, however, it must be stressed, the true name of the dish is pasta with garlic and oil *(aghiue e oghiu)*.

shepherds pasta

Pasta a picurara

A delicate and delicious dish that is in bold contrast to the rough-and-ready lifestyle of shepherds, to whom it is attributed.

Ingredients

1 onion, very finely sliced
Extra-virgin olive oil
1 pound potatoes, peeled and diced
Fresh flat-leaf parsley, chopped
Milk
Sea salt
1 pound *ditalini*
Fresh pecorino, grated

In a large pot, gently fry the onion in olive oil until just beginning to turn golden (it must not brown). Add the diced potatoes, parsley, and enough milk to cover. Bring to a boil, then lower the heat and cook until the potatoes are tender. Salt to taste. The potatoes will gradually absorb most of the milk, but the final presentation should be creamy, not dry.

Cook the pasta in boiling salted water, drain, and transfer to a large serving platter or bowl. Dress with the potato sauce and an abundant amount of pecorino. (The original recipe calls for pecorino *a prima sale*, which is the second stage of curing, between the first stage when the cheese is fresh and milky and before it has been left to age.)

Pasta with Ricotta
Pasta ccâ ricotta

An ancient saying goes: latte di capra, ricotta di pecora, formaggio di vacca, *or "milk from the goat, ricotta from the sheep, cheese from the cow," referring to the best variety of each one can choose.*

Sheep's milk ricotta is, in fact, superior—for taste, texture and the fineness of grain—and is the ricotta of choice when a recipe requires fresh ricotta to be eaten uncooked and flavor is of primary importance.

Ingredients
   1 pound pasta (*ditalini* are ideal)
   3/4 cup ricotta (preferably sheep's milk ricotta)
   Sea salt
   Pecorino with peppercorns

Cook the pasta in boiling salted water and drain, retaining a cup of the water. Put 2 or 3 tablespoons of ricotta per serving into a serving bowl. Add a few teaspoons of pasta water and stir to dissolve the cheese until it becomes smooth and creamy. Mix in a few tablespoons of grated pecorino, then add the pasta. Salt to taste, toss, and serve hot.

PASTA WITH FRIED ZUCCHINI
Pasta ccâ cucuzza fritta

Please use the long thin type of zucchini as this is typical of the south. Today it is overtaking all markets in Italy.

Here it is worthwhile to remember the old saying: falla comu vuoi, zuccaru abbiaccinni na visazza, ma sempri e cucuzza *("prepare squash as you like, throw a sack of sugar over it, but squash it was and squash will remain"). This saying reflects the fact that this humble vegetable has always been considered bland and therefore bereft of any nutritional value. This recipe proves the contrary.*

The fried zucchini also can be served as a side dish, contorno, *with boiled meats or other lean meat.*

Ingredients
    Zucchini
    Extra-virgin olive oil
    Sea salt
    Fresh *caciocavallo ragusano*
    Pasta (thick *spaghettoni* are ideal)

Slice the zucchini into disks no thicker than 1/2 inch and, in a skillet, fry in batches in hot olive oil until golden on both sides. As they cook, set aside and lightly salt.

Meanwhile, bring a large pot of salted water to a boil and cook the pasta until al dente. Drain and transfer to a serving platter.

Toss the cooked pasta with the fried zucchini, along with the oil used to fry them. Top with an abundant grating of *caciocavallo*.

DOGFISH PIE
'Mpanata di palummu

Dogfish (palummu), *the name given to a smaller species of shark, usually grows up to 40 inches in length. For this reason, fishmongers skin it in front of buyers to prove that it is not a "dangerous" shark. Certainly the taste is slightly gamey but quite pleasant and is featured in many recipes. This recipe is from the Vittoria area.*

Ingredients

For the filling

1 onion, chopped finely
1 cup tomato sauce (see page 82)
20 green olives, pitted and roughly
   chopped
Celery heart, chopped
2 tablespoons salted capers, rinsed
Fresh flat-leaf parsley, chopped

Zucchini, sliced into rounds
Sea salt
Pepper
2 pounds dogfish fillets

For the crust

Bread dough
1 egg, beaten

Fry the onion in a large skillet until transparent. When it is done, add tomato sauce, celery heart, olives, capers, parsley, and salt and pepper to taste. Mix well and bring to a boil. Then add the fish fillets and cook for approximately 10 minutes after the pan comes back to a boil. In another skillet, fry the zucchini rounds in olive oil until golden, and salt.

Roll out a simple bread dough (flour, lard, and salt) into a thin sheet. Cut out 2 circles slightly wider than your baking dish. Line the greased deep baking dish with one, making sure the dough overlaps the edges. Pour the fish mixture into the lined dish. Layer the zucchini rounds over the fish mixture. Cover the top of the pie with the other circle of dough, pinching the edges together well. Brush the dough with beaten egg, place in a preheated 350° oven and bake until golden.

In general, fishmongers, to reassure buyers that it is not like the leopard shark (or the *meriglio* or *gattuccio*) remove its skin only at the moment of making the sale. The skin is typically ashen gray with little dark spots unevenly distributed throughout its body. In Sicilian it is also known as *lingua di San Paulu* (Saint Paul's tongue) because of the superstition that carrying a *palummu* tooth safeguards you from the bite of poisonous snakes.

sardines with lettuce
Sardi ccâ lattuca

There are 30 or so different ways of cooking fish, but in Sicily frying is by far the preferred method. An old saying has it that in order to eat good fish you need these "Fs": friscu (fresh), funnu (deep sea), frittu (fried), fora frattaria (not cooked in a hurry), fattu (cooked by someone else!) and francu (preferably received as a gift).

Sardines, in reality the poorest of the so-called "blue fish," can in fact possess almost all the "Fs" but the smell after frying them at home is rather strong and tends to remain for a day at least. And that is why this recipe was invented (it comes from the plains around Ragusa in the Scoglitti area adjacent to the coast)—the use of the lettuce will keep the fish quite moist during cooking and reduce unpleasant odors.

Ingredients
    Sardines, heads removed, scaled and cleaned
    Extra-virgin olive oil
    2 lemons, juiced
    Sea salt
    Black pepper, freshly-ground
    Fresh flat-leaf parsley, chopped
    2 fresh bay leaves, crumbled
    1 head lettuce

Allow the sardines to marinate for at least 1 hour in the olive oil, lemons, salt, pepper, parsley, and bay leaves. Remove the outer leaves of the lettuce, using only the next layer of large leaves and not the heart. Begin layering the fish and lettuce in a large saucepan with a lid, starting with a layer of sardines, laying them split flat like open books. Cover with a layer of lettuce and then another layer of sardines. Continue until all the fish has been used, ending with a layer of lettuce. Cover the saucepan tightly so that the steam cannot escape and cook over a low heat for 45 minutes.

MULLET
Trigghiola

Here we are using very small mullet, barely 2 inches long, which by law can be caught only for a very short period during the year. This contributes to their rarity on the market and the resulting cost. But this dish is quite delicious and the people of Ragusa will go to great lengths to enjoy it once a year.

Three things must be stressed. Mullets demand a frying pan (there are no alternatives or variations). They must be eaten whole, meaning complete with head and bones, given that they are so small and tender. They should be washed in seawater as no further cleaning is required other than perhaps to separate them from small pieces of algae or other extraneous matter.

Ingredients
> Freshly-caught baby mullet
> Flour
> Several tablespoons extra-virgin olive oil
> Sea salt

Set out a plate of flour for dusting. Dust the fish in flour immediately after they have been rinsed, shaking off any excess flour. In a large skillet, heat the olive oil until it is very hot and add the fish. It is important to fry them close together, in single layer (it may be necessary to fry them in batches). The heat of the pan will allow the flour to cement the fish together rather like an frittata.

Once the bottom has become golden, turn over the "frittata" with the help of a saucepan lid and cook on the other side. Place this on a serving dish after salting to taste, and serve hot.

TUNA WITH ZUCCHINI
Tunnina ccâ cucuzza

Sicilians use a great deal of tuna, and over the entire island this much-appreciated fish—with its flesh, firm and consistent, without very much in the way of bones—lends itself to being prepared in many different ways. This recipe is quite unique, coming only from the Vittoria area. Note, however, that it is really a continuation of tuna fried with oregano (below) in order to use up whatever may be left over.

Tuna with Oregano

Ingredients
> Slices of tuna
> Extra-virgin olive oil
> Fresh oregano leaves
> Sea salt

Coat the bottom of a skillet with olive oil and fry the tuna until golden (without using any flour). Once each piece is cooked on all sides, sprinkle with abundant oregano and salt, and serve very hot.

Tuna with Zucchini

If any of the fish is left, it would be very difficult to use it by re-frying or heating, so this recipe has been devised for this purpose.

Ingredients
> 1/2 onion, finely sliced
> 1 1/2 cups tomatoes, peeled, seeded, and chopped
> Zucchini, peeled and diced
> Sea salt
> Pepper
> Slices of tuna, diced

Put in a skillet the finely-sliced onion, tomatoes, and zucchini. Salt and pepper to taste. Cook the three vegetables until the zucchini is cooked through and the sauce has somewhat condensed. Once this is done, add the cooked pieces of fish and warm through gently for approximately 10 minutes.

STUFFED POULTRY
Jaddina china

*A dish served on grand occasions, particularly for the Feast of the Patron Saint,
St. Giovanni in Ragusa, and at Christmas and New Year's Eve elsewhere.*

Ingredients

For the stuffing

6 ounces chicken hearts and livers, minced
6 ounces ground beef
1/2 onion, finely chopped
Pepper
Fresh flat-leaf parsley, chopped
Fresh basil leaves
2 cloves garlic, minced
3/4 cup rice
3 to 4 ounces *caciocavallo ragusano,* grated
2 eggs, beaten
Bread crumbs

Hen, rooster, or capon, deboned,
about 4 1/2 pounds
1 cup extra-virgin olive oil
Sea salt
Red wine
Beef or chicken stock

In a large bowl, mix the minced chicken livers and hearts with the ground beef, onion, pepper, parsley, basil, and garlic.

In a large saucepan, boil the rice until cooked al dente, then fold the first mixture into this along with the *caciocavallo,* eggs, and bread crumbs to bind. Mix until it is well-blended and forms a soft stuffing. Stuff the cavity of the bird with this, and sew up with a large needle and twine.

Place the bird in a large roasting pan, baste with a glass of olive oil, and sew it closed on both sides. Salt to taste. Roast the chicken gently in a preheated 325° oven, adding enough red wine during the roasting so it does not dry out. Finally, add 2 ladles of stock during cooking. Cook for at least 90 minutes.

Lamb with Cheese Glaze Agnieddu agglassatu

The *agglassatu* is one of the most typical dishes of the eastern part of Sicily and its originality is derived from a particular method of preparation. Once lamb has been braised with onion, olive oil, and pepper, and wedges of potato have been added halfway through cooking, the resulting gravy—and here lies the secret—is enriched with abundant grated cheese which is allowed to melt gradually as the pan is removed from the heat, forming a particularly delicious sauce, or glaze, the *glassatu*.

Skylarks with Onion Beccaficu nna cipudda

In the famous dinner of the Roman Trimalcione [a character in Petronius' *Satyricon*], a dish of small game birds stuffed into eggs was served. This is something analogous. Once, when plump skylarks were available, they were stuffed into onions and cooked whole, without their heads and feathers, the onions being emptied of their centers for the purpose. They were sprinkled with salt, pepper, and oregano, and their onion casings were roasted on the grill and cooked until perfect. The grilled onion gave the skylark an excellent taste. But this was Once Upon a Time, when skylarks were available.

Stuffed Pork Ribs Cuosti chini

We are talking about whole pork spareribs still on the bone and "stuffed" by making an incision between the bone and the meat to form a "pouch" into which the stuffing could be introduced. According to individual taste, a stuffing is prepared comprising some if not all of the following: bread crumbs, herbs, ground pork, and cheese. The aperture is closed by binding the rib cutlet and it is cooked by frying quickly in very hot oil. This specialty, by now known all over Italy, originated in Chiaramonte Gulfi.

pork in gelatin
Jlatina di maiali

This is an ancient specialty of the Ragusa area, which later spread to Catania, where it is called suzu *or* susu. *Originally conceived as a means of using the inedible parts of the pig such as the feet, the head, and skin, these were made more palatable with the addition of a natural, spicy gelatin. In later times, due to the relative increase in economic prosperity, pieces of lean meat were also added to enrich the dish.*

Everyone has a recipe—every home, every butcher (the gelatina *was available in butcher shops originally), each restaurant. The following is a typical modern-day recipe. You can use the following recipe incorporating any pieces of pork in any proportion that suits you.*

Ingredients
    Pork, see below
    4 bay leaves
    1/2 cup red wine vinegar
    Peperoncino, hot red chili pepper, 1 teaspoon chopped [or dried flakes]
    3 bitter oranges
    Juice of 3 or 4 lemons
    Sea salt

Boil the following together in at least 10 quarts of water: about 6 to 7 pounds of meat roughly chopped but in large pieces, 2 trotters split in half lengthwise, a piece of pig head, 1 pound pork skin well-scraped and cleaned, salt to taste (be careful, as the resulting broth will reduce to half), bay leaves, and chili. Boil for 1 hour over very low heat, then remove the head and the feet. (Leave the skin to cook until the liquid has reduced by half before removing it.)

Some people like to discard the skin, but if you wish to use it, the fat must be scraped away leaving only the skin, which is then chopped finely and added back to the pot.

Filter the broth obtained and season further with wine vinegar, orange and lemon juices (the "bitter" element in this dish is according to personal taste). But it is good to keep in mind that the resulting gelatin must have a certain amount of flavor.

Once the broth has cooled, remove the film of fat that has formed on the surface. Put the meat into individual molds. Pour the liquid into these molds and refrigerate until the gelatin has formed completely. The finished gelatinized meats are removed from the molds by turning them upside down onto plates. Serve sprinkled with chopped chili.

Variation

If obtaining a part of a head and the feet, which are the natural source of the gelatin, is impossible, you can add sheets or packets of dried gelatin manufactured commercially.

Braised Lamb in Bread 'Mpanata d'agnieddu

A traditional Easter dish that is always included on everyone's holiday table. The lamb is stewed then braised with bones or without, and with potatoes or without (the latter dishes belonging to *cucina povera,* peasant cookery, while the former are part of a richer cuisine). The braise is then encased in pieces of bread dough with onion, parsley, and whatever herbs take your fancy, placed in the oven [on a greased baking sheet] and baked briefly until done. Enjoy it hot.

Easter Pastries
Pastieri o Pastieri di Pasqua

Another rather complex preparation (but one that is well worthwhile) that originated in the Ragusa area, particularly in the plains. These pouches are filled with a rich stuffing but open on top. The stuffing is made up of internal parts, which are also traditional at Easter.

Ingredients

For the pastry	For the filling
1/3 cup lard	Extra-virgin olive oil
2 pounds flour	2 cloves garlic, chopped
Salt	1 1/4 pounds livers (lamb and/or goat)
Water	1 pound chopped meat, optional
	Fresh flat-leaf parsley, chopped
	Sea salt
	Pepper
	Juice of 2 lemons
	5 tablespoons fresh *caciocavallo ragusano*
	1 egg, beaten

Make a plain pastry using lard, flour, salt, and water, and let the dough rest for at least 2 hours. (You can substitute plain bread dough, enriching it a little with some olive oil.)

Make the filling by very lightly browning the garlic in olive oil in a skillet, and then adding the chopped lamb or goat livers, with small pieces of chopped meat if you like. Add parsley, and salt and pepper to taste. Cook until the meat begins to take on the flavor of the garlic and parsley, then mix in the lemon juice. Allow to cool. When the filling is cool, add the *caciocavallo* and blend well.

Roll out the pastry into thin sheets and cut out 5-inch circles, then place a spoonful of the filling in the centers. Using your hands, roll the dough around the filling into a cylinder shape, curling one edge closed. Fill these until they are very full to the brim. Brush with the beaten egg. Place the pies on a greased baking sheet and bake in a preheated 350° oven until golden brown.

RAGUSAN MEATBALLS
Purpetti di maiali e Purpetti ccâ sarsa

Finally, it's time to discuss meatballs. Sicilians love meatballs so much there is no food they have not shaped into balls—meat (exceptional are the meatballs made from wild hare and wild rabbit); fish (ball-shaped sardines are classics); vegetables (eggplant, potatoes, mushrooms, and artichokes); and even certain sweets, which are referred to as "sweet" meatballs.

It is said that the meat grinder was invented in Sicily so that Sicilians could eat beef (as cows and oxen generally were beasts of burden and working animals, and their meat known to be tough and leathery). To be sure, meatballs are prepared at home, not in restaurants, where they are never made: Sicilians are suspicious by nature.

Ingredients

1 onion, finely chopped	Sea salt
Fresh flat-leaf parsley, chopped	Pepper
2 or 3 cloves garlic, finely chopped	2 to 3 tablespoons fresh *caciocavallo ragusano*
1 pound ground pork	Extra-virgin olive oil
2 eggs	1 tablespoon bread crumbs, optional
1 tablespoon red wine	Milk, optional

After chopping the onion, parsley, and garlic, combine them with the ground pork in a mixing bowl. Incorporate the eggs into the mixture, then red wine, salt and pepper to taste, and *caciocavallo.* Take small amounts and form them into the shape of meatballs (walnut size oval-shaped balls, not too thick, and do not flatten them). Fry them in a large skillet in boiling olive oil until they obtain the typical bronze color.

They must be eaten very hot. If cold, they lose their aroma and the crispness of the outside.

Variations
The initial mixture for the meatballs can be made thicker with the addition of bread crumbs or softer with the addition of a little milk.

Purpetti ccâ sarsa
But here is the way to eat leftovers. Use a good tomato sauce (see page 82) and heat the meatballs immersed for about 20 minutes. And there you have another way to enjoy this special dish.

HOLIDAY RAGÙ
Rau dî festi

Once again pork and tomato combine to give us a culinary masterpiece from Ragusa. There is a very good reason why this dish is designated dî festi, *meaning "of feast days," due to the complexity of its preparation, the amount of time needed indicating the importance of the occasion, and its grandiose presentation. To prepare this dish used to be equivalent of receiving a "laurea," a university degree, in cooking for the mistress of the house. Today, all traces of it have been lost — it is too complex, too much work, and too time-consuming.*

Ingredients

1 pound potatoes, cut into chunks
1 pound Ragusan sausage
1 onion, finely sliced
4 tablespoons extra-virgin olive oil
2 tablespoons *strattu* (tomato extract)
    diluted with 1 teaspoon of red wine
1 1/2 pounds tomatoes, peeled
    and chopped
Sea salt
Pepper

2 fresh bay leaves, crumbled
2 cloves
Cinnamon
2 pounds *falsumauru* (see page 93)
A marrowbone
12 pork meatballs (see previous recipe)
3/4 cup fresh peas
Fresh basil leaves
1 teaspoon sugar

In a large skillet, fry the potatoes and sprinkle with salt. In another skillet, coil the sausages and fry them until cooked on both sides. Set these aside. Have the *falsumauru* ready.

In a wide heavy-bottomed pot, fry the onion in olive oil. Add the tomato extract. As soon as the wine evaporates, add tomatoes, salt and pepper to taste, bay leaves, cloves, and a pinch of cinnamon. Bring to the sauce to a boil and simmer for 10 minutes. Then set the *falsumauru* in the center along with a marrowbone and sausages, and put the pork meatballs around the edges.

Add enough water to cover all and bring this to a boil. Cover the pot, lowering the heat, and simmer for 2 hours. At this point, add fresh peas and the fried potatoes and sprinkle with sugar. Adjust the seasoning and continue cooking for another 30 minutes.

On a large serving platter, arrange this for presentation—place the *falsumauru* in the center surrounded by the sausages, meatballs, potatoes and peas, with the sauce poured over all. And the bone? Give it to the dog.

RABBIT STEW
Sarmuggi a vitturisa

What is called carmùci *in the Catania area is called* sarmuggi *in Ragusa. After some investigation, I discovered that both words derive from the Persian* kharmush *or* kharmus *which mean, respectively, mouse and big mouse. The Arabs used the same word to describe a variety of fig tree that was small and immature. The term then passed into the vocabulary of Calabria, where* caramuscia *designates a small boy, not so much for his age but for his inability to grow. With more searching, I found that in the Italian of the 1600s the word* caromogio *referred to a "small, deformed person."*

The sarmuggi *in our recipe is a small rabbit, found among the newborn, and therefore big as a large mouse and similar to it for the color of its coat and its quickness. Today, wild rabbits are a rarity, but once the area was so abundant with them that cooks invented many specialties to alter the taste. Don't be discouraged—you can use this recipe with commercially raised rabbits.*

Ingredients

1 rabbit, cleaned and quartered
1/2 cup extra-virgin olive oil
Several cups water
Fresh flat-leaf parsley, chopped
Fresh herb leaves, finely chopped:
   mint, basil, sage, rosemary, oregano
1 carrot, finely chopped
1 celery heart, finely chopped

1 clove garlic, finely chopped
1 onion, finely chopped
3/4 cup tomatoes, peeled and roughly chopped
Sea salt
Pepper
Red wine

Arrange the rabbit parts in a small baking dish and cover with the olive oil and enough water to immerse the meatier parts of the rabbit. Place in a preheated 400° oven for 10 minutes, then remove from the heat, turn the pieces and return to the oven for another 15 minutes. Remove the dish from the oven again and add all the herbs and vegetables, tomatoes, and salt and pepper to taste. Oil the pieces well and return the dish to the oven, lowering the temperature so the rabbit continues to cook at 350° for another 30 minutes. After that, sprinkle the rabbit pieces with red wine and cook for a final 10 minutes while the wine is evaporating.

TRIPE RAGUSA-STYLE
Trippa a rausana

An ancient dish from the Iblei Mountain area, a real delicacy for those who are fond of tripe.

Ingredients
    2 tablespoons extra-virgin olive oil
    1 tablespoon lard
    2 pounds tripe, washed, dried, and cut into strips
    Sea salt
    Pepper
    1 quart beef stock
    1 medium eggplant, peeled and cut lengthwise into strips
    1 cup tomato sauce
    2 to 4 teaspoons *caciocavallo ragusano,* grated
    1 tablespoon almonds, roasted and chopped
    1 tablespoon walnuts, chopped
    Cinnamon
    1/2 teaspoon sugar

In a large skillet, heat the oil and lard until smoking hot. Add the tripe strips along with salt and pepper to taste and stir for a few minutes, then add enough stock to cover. Simmer for 1 hour.

Fry the eggplant until golden in another skillet. As soon as the tripe is cooked (there should be very little liquid remaining), add the tomato sauce, cooked eggplant, *caciocavallo,* almonds, walnuts, a pinch of cinnamon, and sugar. Stir to combine and continue stirring for another 10 minutes. Adjust the seasoning and serve hot.

wrapped beef intestines
Turcinuna

It would appear that this term is derived from the Italian torcere *(twist) or* ritorcere *(twist again) due to the technique of coiling something around the beef entrails in preparation for grilling. This is also a specialty during the Easter period. The internal organs could not go to waste, naturally.*

Ingredients
>   Beef intestines, cut into strips
>   Large spring onions or small leeks
>   Extra-virgin olive oil
>   Small onions, finely chopped
>   Fresh flat-leaf parsley, chopped
>   2 to 3 cloves garlic, chopped
>   Sea salt
>   Pepper
>   Juice of a lemon, optional

Wash the intestines thoroughly, with the final rinse under running water. Wrap each length around a large spring onion or small leek, after removing the roots and most of the green leaves. Place these in a large saucepan with olive oil and arrange them tightly on all sides to keep from unfolding.

Add the small onions along with parsley, garlic, salt and pepper. Allow to cook for a few minutes on high heat, then add a glass of water. Cook until the water has completely evaporated. Once the oil begins to sizzle, turn the meat until it is golden all over. The *turcinuna* are ready to serve immediately. You may sprinkle lemon juice over them if you like.

snails
Babbaluci rianati

In summer, there are hundreds of little pale white snails to be found in the fields clinging to stalks of fennel or wheat before the harvest.

A Sicilian proverb that hardly needs to be interpreted tells you how many snails man can eat: vavaluci a sucari e fimmini a vasari, nun puonnu mai stancari (two things you never tire of, sucking up snails and kissing women).

Ingredients
Snails
Extra-virgin olive oil
Sea salt
Fresh oregano, chopped
Spring onions with a long stems

The snails will not need purging, once they are collected, if they are still dormant and still have the small protective membranes over their openings. Place them in a saucepan with some tepid water on moderate heat. Once they begin to emerge, bring this to a boil and continue boiling for 10 minutes.

In a tureen, add olive oil, salt, an abundant amount of oregano, and spring onions. Drain the snails and add them to the tureen, stirring vigorously to ensure that they are thoroughly coated in the oil and herbs. Serve hot.

I have already provided a list of the most common snails consumed in Sicily (see "Neither Fish Nor Fowl" in the Catania section). I will simply add that people fed on snails since ancient times. Pliny said, "they comfort the stomach provided you eat them in odd numbers." In several Italian regions, it is common to indulge on snails during feasts such as the one for St. Giovanni both in Lazio and in Sicily. In Sicily however, they are often cooked *picchi pacchi* style, with a light sauce of tomatoes and onions. Snails are also consumed in great quantities in Radicofani in Tuscany, for the feast of Saints Peter and Paul. We have not been able to find out the significance of the connection between snails and saints.

RIVER CRAB STOCK
Granci di sciumi

River crabs, by now, are a rarity for a variety of reasons: low rainfall and the widespread exploitation of subterranean water reserves for irrigation purposes, not to mention the pollution of the few water resources that remain.

Crabs, therefore, have very little environment left where they can survive. To think that once, and I remember it well, little boys in the Ippari River valley went crab hunting and brought their catch back hanging from poles to sell to avid customers. I remember also how peasants gathered buckets of crabs in the Dirillo River valley immediately after a summer thunderstorm, when the crabs, perhaps frightened by the thunder, came out of their hiding places. The peasants along the banks of the Irminio River easily caught the crabs by using a particularly unusual bait. They placed a bone with a little meat on it, or a piece of tuna, outside the burrows the crabs lived in, enticing them.

But how much substance is there, actually, in a crab, even if it is a large one? A Sicilian proverb provides the answer: rizzi, pateddi e granci, assai spenni e nenti manci (sea urchins, limpets and crabs —you spend a lot, but eat not much). There is only one way to make a meal of either freshwater crabs or the marine variety and that is to make a consommé of them, as in the following recipe.

Ingredients

2 pounds live crabs	Sea salt
2 mature tomatoes, chopped	Pepper
1/2 onion, chopped	Extra-virgin olive oil
2 cloves garlic, chopped	Fresh basil leaves
1 celery leaf	

The live crabs must be well washed (careful of the claws!) and then must be dropped into a stockpot of boiling water. Leave them in the pot until they are finished cooking. Remove the pot from heat. When the water has cooled enough to handle them, remove the crabs and crush them with a mortar and pestle or by some other method to crack the shells and the claws. Then put the tomatoes, garlic, onion, celery leaf, and salt and pepper to taste into the stockpot. Add the crabs. Cook for at least 1 hour, then strain all the solids from the broth obtained.

You can use this stock for whatever purpose you see fit: to cook *pastina,* small pasta; to make risotto; or to serve as soup. In any case, some fresh basil will enhance the flavor.

CAROB MUSHROOMS
Funci di carrùa

There is not a single trace of this mushroom in any of the hundreds of texts that discuss, illustrate, and describe mushrooms. It seems that for science they don't even exist.

Very few indeed even recognize the carob tree that grows in the Siracusa area and the area around Ragusa. This mushroom grows in the trunk of the carob tree towards the base and is similar in appearance to fistulacea hepatica in its shapeless mass. When it emerges it has a whitish compact mass, which tends to grow increasingly yellow as it ages, until it turns rosy white upon maturity. It normally appears in the warmer months between July and August. Owing to its rarity, there is no market price on it. Therefore, the lucky person who finds one will often sit patiently under the tree for a few days, waiting for it to mature and become even more precious.

Some specimens can weigh over 2 pounds, but keep in mind that the newborn mushrooms are the ones that afford the most exceptional taste. In fact, the older they get, the tougher they are and their taste blander. There is not a variety of recipes for cooking this fungus—everyone prepares it a spezzatino (stewed).

Ingredients

1/2 onion, chopped	Fresh flat-leaf parsley, chopped
Extra-virgin olive oil	1 bay leaf, crumbled
1 pound carob mushrooms	Sea salt
1 clove garlic, chopped	Pepper
3 ripe tomatoes, peeled, seeded, and chopped	1/2 cup water

Chop the mushrooms into large pieces. In a large skillet, fry the onion in olive oil until golden, then add the mushrooms and garlic. Stir a few minutes to blend. Add the tomatoes, parsley, bay leaf, salt and pepper to taste, then half glass of water. Cover and simmer over very low heat for 30 minutes.

MUSHROOM BALLS
Purpetti di funci

In Vittoria's pine grove, where the very last Aleppo pines survive, and in Chiaramonte Gulfi, you can still find the pine mushroom (lactarius deliciosis), *known by its dialect name* funciu di pinu. *These grow at the feet of the pine trees, look like small, greenish porcini mushrooms, and have the characteristic resinous flavor of their pine environment. At the time when they are most abundant, they are cooked in various ways. The following is one of the most unusual recipes.*

Ingredients
    2 pounds pine mushrooms
    3 cloves garlic, chopped
    Fresh flat-leaf parsley, chopped
    2 eggs, beaten, in separate bowls
    Sea salt
    Pepper
    2 cups bread crumbs
    Extra-virgin olive oil

Clean the mushrooms carefully under running water. Toss them into a stockpot of lightly-salted boiling water. Allow to boil for 10 minutes, then remove from the heat and drain them. Once they have cooled, transfer to a bowl and mash them into a purée. Add the garlic, parsley, 1 beaten egg, and salt and pepper to taste. Mix in enough bread crumbs to make a paste suitable to form into balls.

Make small balls with the mixture and dip them in the second beaten egg, then roll them in bread crumbs. In a heavy-bottomed pot, deep-fry them in very hot olive oil until they are golden.

Variation
The mushroom balls can be fried directly in olive oil without the egg and bread crumbs.

WILD asparagus
Spàraci sarbàgghi

While everyone is familiar with the commercially grown asparagus, few know the wild version, known in dialect as sarbàgghi *(wild), which people name variously according to the locality—from* spàraci di muntagna *(mountain asparagus) to* sparacogna. *There are several different species, ranging from the pastel green* A. acutifolius *to the darker green* A. tenuifolius *whose stalks verge on black. Both are similar, as their stalks are very slender indeed. They grow spontaneously in the woodlands among oaks and in the undergrowth among the rocks.*

Asparagus hunters, usually farmers, gather them and tie them in bunches, selling them for a good price by the roadside from January well into the spring. These asparagus have a rather bitter taste, but can be most pleasant when prepared properly in the kitchen. They can be served stewed, as in the following recipe, can be used as a dressing for spaghetti, or added to a risotto or an omelette.

Ingredients
- 1 pound wild asparagus
- 2 cloves garlic, finely chopped
- Fresh flat-leaf parsley, chopped
- Extra-virgin olive oil
- Sea salt
- Pepper

Wash the asparagus, discarding the hard part of the stems near the bottom. You only want the tender part of the stalks. (You can test for tenderness with a fingernail that will tell you when the stalk is unable to be pierced.) Put them into a wide saucepan with garlic, parsley, a little oil, and salt and pepper to taste. Add a few tablespoons of water and simmer for no more than 15 minutes or until tender.

cheese

A discussion on varieties of cheese typical of the Ragusa area would have to be a long one, such is the quality and variety of the types available on the market. But I will limit myself to a single item: *caciocavallo*. This cheese has been produced in the region since ancient times. It was given the European Union Protected Denomination of Origin stamp of recognition (see page 143) as a typical product of the area only recently and is marketed with the name of *ragusano*. Among the best are the ones from Ragusa and Modica.

In the plains, however, various pecorino (sheep's milk) cheeses are produced, and a delicious ricotta that you can buy directly from the herdsman.

fried bread and eggs
Pani frittu ccû l'ova

There are some recipes in cucina povera *that perform several useful functions while providing a very pleasant dining experience. The following recipe is a good example of being both easy to make and a good way to use whatever might be left from another meal. It makes a quick lunch and although it is filling, it is also nutritious, providing a good balance between fats and carbohydrates. It costs little and it tastes good. What more could you ask for?*

Ingredients
    Several cups dry bread, cut up
    Several eggs, beaten
    Sea salt
    Pepper

Sprinkle the bread pieces with a little water if it is very dry. In a skillet, fry the bread pieces quickly with a little olive oil. Beat the eggs in a bowl with a little salt then slide the fried bread pieces in, making sure each piece is well coated with egg. Return to the skillet until the eggs set.

EGGS WITH Basil
Piscirova ccû basilicò*

This is the second time that we encounter the term piscirova, *which could be translated as "eggs that have been fried like fish." We are talking about an extremely common dish in Sicily, the frittata, using eggs and one other ingredient that characterizes it. Ingredient amounts depend on servings. The potato frittata is one classic—cut potatoes into discs, fry them in olive oil, and then cover them with eggs. Others are made with artichokes, zucchini, tomato sauce, and so on. In our coverage of the cooking of Sicily, we come across many frittata, including the following from Ragusa that is among the simplest. It is made ever more fragrant by the use of basil.*

Ingredients
> 6 eggs
> 3 tablespoons *caciocavallo ragusano*
> Bread crumbs
> Several fresh basil leaves, torn
> Pepper
> Sea salt
> 2 tablespoons extra-virgin olive oil

Beat the eggs together with a pinch of salt. Add the *caciocavallo,* some bread crumbs, basil, and salt and pepper to taste. In a skillet with a lid, heat the olive oil until it is hot and pour in the egg mixture.

Meanwhile, heat the skillet lid in the oven until it is quite hot. Cover the skillet with this lid. Lower the flame and shake the skillet to loosen the eggs from time to time. Turn the frittata using the saucepan lid and cook on the second side until done.

*The name is derived from the Greek *basilikòn* and in Sicilian it is still pronounced with the accent on the final vowel, *basilicò.* Until a few decades ago, a beautiful basil plant adorned with a red bow would be sent on the Feast Day of Saint Giovanni, June 24, to the person chosen to become godfather to one's child. Whoever received the gift would indicate acceptance of the new bond by sending back a gift.

fruits

THE province of Ragusa is not particularly rich in fruit, if one excludes table grapes and apricots. It has an immense output of vegetables produced under cover in special greenhouses. The vegetable market at Vittoria actually exports twenty-five percent of Italy's needs for these products. It is worthwhile, however, to remember the region does produce bananas along the coastline; sour cherries, cherries, quinces, arbutus, mullberries, pomegranates, Japanese medlar fruit, and loquats; and in the winter, plums. The fruit that must never be missing from the Christmas table, one of the "seven fruits," is the myrtle berry. In the countryside there are masses of blackberries growing wild.

sweets

Ragusa has typical, traditional production of sweets, some of which are unique and not found in other parts of Sicily. Certain sweets have been in the region for centuries, going back to those prepared in honor of special occasions and Feast Days that occurred annually and that are still offered today. With certain practical changes to suit the times, they are still recognizable, much to the delight of the traditionalists. I give the recipes for some of these, but it is worthwhile noting some for which I do not, such as the chocolate from Modica,* the *minni chini* (filled

There are no towns or villages that do not possess mulberry trees: even the state road from Vittoria to Comiso is lined with beautiful white mulberry trees that are remaining examples of an important component in the breeding of silk worms. The black mulberry tree is usually found in courtyards where they provide much happiness to children who will soil their clothes with red stains and distress to their mothers who have to clean clothes and children.

*It is not clear why one of the first chocolate factories was begun in Modica in 1700. The cocoa seeds were the starting point of the process then. Now they start from the bitter cocoa plant. The rest of the process was done by hand with wooden tools and on lava stone surfaces where the mixture was made, adding sugar, then mixing it well on low heat. The resulting product was a different, leaner, and grainy chocolate because the sugar crystals did not dissolve in the low heat whose purpose was simply to soften the cocoa butter, making it easier to blend. Vanilla or cinnamon was added to give the chocolate

breasts) that are made at Modica for the Feast of St. Agatha; the *mustazzola* made with *vinu cottu* that are typical of Vittoria, Acate, and Comiso; the *petrafennula* (or *aranciata* and *citrata*) made with strips of citrus peel that are cooked in honey until they are candied and hard like a rock, from which they derive their name; and the splendid white *turruni/torrone* (nougat) from Giarratana. But how many more?

Cubbaita o Giuggiulena

THIS is a crisp candy made predominantly with sesame seeds as the main ingredient, with the addition of toasted almonds, that is cooked in honey until it reaches the consistency of *turruni* (*torrone* in Italian). It is then spread out on a marble slab as it cools and is cut into rectangles that are then covered with sugar sprinkles.

Cuddurèddi e Cudduriddùzzi

THESE are typically made at grape harvest time: the first are like little lasagne or gnocchi made from a special dough that is then boiled in *musto* (grape must), while the second are pastries shaped like boats that are also boiled in *mosto* andfinished off with crushed toasted almonds and sugar.

Mosto (GRAPE MUST)

IT is time to explain exactly what *mosto* is, having encountered it in Messina, where it is the base of *vinu cottu*, see page 74, and in Siracusa in the making of *mustata*, see page 118. As soon as wine grapes have been pressed, some of the the first pressing is removed and immediately boiled to halt fermentation. Once it has boiled, it is taken off the heat and a handful of wood ash is added to help sweeten it and to sink any small particles floating in the liquid. This is allowed to sit for a day and is then filtered. Thus we have the *mosto di base* that can be kept for some time in the refrigerator for multiple future uses such as in *mustata* (a method of preserving fruit) or in *vinu cottu* as we have seen.

aroma. It's possible to visit the museum housed in the Palazzo dei Mercedari in Modica to admire, among the many other beautiful things, the workroom of an ancient pastry shop that has been perfectly reconstructed with all the original tools of the time, including those used in the preparation of chocolate.

The term *giuggiulena* (or *giurgiulena*) has come down to us from the Indian language where sesame is still called *gingelli* and *gingil* that became *juliulena* around 1300. Others claim it comes from the Arabic that identifies the seeds as *giolgiolan*. The other term equivalent to this, even though it was derived from the Arabic *qobbait* and *qubbata*, is actually from a Greek word, *koptè* (and then from the Latin *coba*). These names identified a focaccia made with flour and sesame seed. In short, we can conclude that in eastern Sicily the name *giuggiulena* applies both to the sesame seed and the biscotti made from it. In western Sicily, however, *giuggiulena* identifies the seeds, but the biscotti is called *cobbàita*.

'Mpanatigghi

This is a very ancient and very curious recipe from Modica, jealously guarded by the few who know it. It is a sweet pastry that has meat among its ingredients!

Ingredients

> 5 cups flour
> 1 3/4 cups sugar
> 1 cup lard
> 3 eggs
> 1 tablespoon ammonia for sweets [baking powder]
> 1/2 cup dry white wine
> Milk
>
> *Filling*
> 1 pound veal
> 1/2 cup lard
> 7 ounces (3/4 cup) unsweetened chocolate
> 1 cup sugar
> Cinnamon
> Cloves
> Confectioners' sugar

Combine the flour, sugar, lard, eggs, baking powder, wine, and enough milk to make a stiff dough, then set aside.

The filling is prepared with veal that has been lightly fried in some lard and, once cooled, removed and minced finely. Returning this to the same pan, add chocolate, sugar, cinnamon, and cloves. Mix completely until the chocolate and sugar have dissolved, then remove the pan from the heat.

Roll out the pastry very fine (about 1/4 inch thick) and then cut out 4-inch circles. Place some filling on each and fold over as if making ravioli, sealing the edges. With the tip of a knife, make a small incision in the shape of a cross in the top of each. Place the pastries on a greased baking sheet and bake in a preheated 350° oven until they begin to brown. Dust with confectioners' sugar while they are still hot.

The history of these sweets is a bit strange if you consider that in spite of the fact that they contain meat, they were created for the period of Lent. The sisters of the Convent of the Origlione in Palermo and those of the Convent of Modica, working in perfect harmony, probably the result of cultural and gastronomic exchanges, made these pastries as a labor of charity.

It was customary for large groups of preachers to travel from one end of Sicily to the other to prepare people for the Precept and to perform their spiritual exercises during the forty days of the Lenten penitence. The preachers, fatigued by their long journeys and their equally long sermons, tired and hungry from their Lenten fasting, must have inspired pity in the nuns who invented these restorative and energy-giving desserts for them. We don't know if the preachers knew beforehand the contents of the pastries, but one thing is certain—they were refreshed, restored and given new energy.

Mucatuli o nucatoli

This recipe seems to have originated in the Convent of St. Elizabeth in Palermo and was typical at Christmas throughout Sicily, but now it seems to exist principally in the Province of Ragusa.

Etymologists do not agree on the origins of the word. Some claim it is derives from the Latin word for walnut, nucatus, *because walnuts were included in the dough. Others claim it comes from the Arabic word* naqal, *meaning dried fruit, which gives a hint as to the ingredients of the filling, which is also very different from family to family.*

Ingredients

4 1/2 cups flour	*Filling*
4 egg yolks	Chopped almonds
1 cup lard	Dried figs, chopped
1 cup sugar	Honey
	Vinu cottu
	Cinnamon

Prepare the dough. Combine and knead with flour, egg yolks, lard, sugar, and enough water to make a stiff dough. Roll it out and cut rectangles measuring 2 by 3 inches.

The filling, which must be quite solid, can be made by combining any or all of the following ingredients according to personal taste: almonds, dried figs, honey, *vinu cottu,* and cinnamon. Place a spoon of filling on each rectangle. These are closed (but not completely) by twisting the sides together so that they form an S shape.

Place on a greased baking sheet and bake in a preheated 400° oven until they begin to brown. They can be glazed according to preference.

Pignuccata

Pignulata and a related recipe, pignuccata, *have similar names and both are made with little balls bound together. But in the sweet we saw in Messina, the* pignulata, *these little balls were baked in the oven. The* pignuccata, *a less refined sweet, though very pleasing, is fried. The part of the name they share, the* pignu, *comes from the tradition of assembling the little balls to resemble a pine cone.*

It is a Carnevale sweet that is made traditionally in Furci Siculo, Buscemi, Ragusa and other places in the Ragusa province such as Santa Croce Camerina, where it is called cicirieddi *because it resembles chickpeas. This sweet is always made for the Feast of St. Joseph.*

Ingredients
    2 cups flour
    7 whole eggs
    5 egg yolks
    1 1/2 ounces liquor [clear, distilled]
    Extra-virgin olive oil
    1/4 cup sugar
    5 egg whites, beaten
    Grated zest of 1 lemon

Make a dough with flour, whole eggs, and egg yolks (but no water). Add the liquor drop by drop to the mixture. Knead well, divide the dough, and roll out into thin log shapes like *grissini*. Slice these across to make small dice then roll them in your hands to make small balls, about 1/2 inches wide. Fry them in a heavy-bottomed pot in very hot oil until they are golden.

Meanwhile, in a small pot, melt the sugar until it caramelizes. Toss the pastry balls briefly in this caramel, drain and mound them on a serving dish in the form of a pinecone.

Dissolve some sugar in water and add this to 5 egg whites, beaten until they form stiff peaks, then add the lemon zest. Pour this quickly over the assembled dessert letting it run down from the top.

Variations
There are many. One calls for the pastry balls to be dipped in honey instead of the caramelized sugar; another does not include the egg whites poured over the top at the end, and so on.

sweet potato fritters
Sfinci di patati aruci

Notice that it is not enough to say sfinci di patati, *but we must add the word* aruci (sweet) *to make clear what is coming and prepare diners for the taste experience. In Ragusa, these are usually made for the Feast of San Martino, when many other kinds of fritters—both sweet and salted—are made.*

Ingredients
> 1 pound potatoes
> 6 cups flour
> Sea salt
> 1 cup sugar
> 2 ounces (4 tablespoons) brewers' yeast
> Extra virgin olive oil
> Sugar for dusting

Boil the potatoes, peel, and mash them. Add the flour, salt, sugar, and brewers' yeast diluted in tepid water. The dough should be quite damp and limp. Knead well and allow to rest for a few of hours.

Once the dough has risen, form fritters by the spoonful and deep-fry the *sfinci* in a pot of boiling olive oil. Once they are golden, remove with a slotted spoon, drain, and dust with abundant sugar.

Variations
All variations are relative to the quantities. Some use 2 pounds potatoes, 3 cups flour, 1/2 cup sugar, with the addition of 2 egg yolks, and the grated zest of a lemon. Others use 2 pounds potatoes, 6 cups flour, 2 cups sugar, and 5 eggs as well. Some prefer to boil these in lard rather than olive oil.

ragusa wines and liqueurs

wines

One of the pearls of Sicilian oenology, *Cerasuolo di Vittoria*, has been a *Denominazione di Origine Controllata (DOC)* wine, or Wine of Designated Origin, since 1968. [And more recently it has earned the DOCG, indicating a very significant wine.] It is produced in modest quantities. Land available is a major factor, given that much of Ragusa is used for the cultivation of more profitable crops. The minimum alcoholic content is thirteen percent. On the label, along with the name *Cerasuolo di Vittoria*, are also the various vineyards that produce it—for example my own winery, Villa Fontane.

There are also other various table wines produced in the area, in different versions (rosé, white, and red) called *Casameno, Cortese, Dalle Terre di Herea*, and *Milaro*.

Two splendid after dinner wines are the *Moscato* and the *Solicchiato*, as well as two others, this time for meditation purposes called the *Perpetuo*, produced at Villa Fontane, and the *Stravecchio Siciliano*. This completes the picture of wines in the Ragusa area.

In the Ragusa area there are no good years, nor bad ones. The peasants, who are descendants of the ancient Ibleans, don't waste time pondering Noah's Ark or the rainbow to forecast the weather. Fortunately for them the weather, the climate, and the air are always favorable, by the grace of God.

The Italian government has identified and awarded the DOC to unique and significant wines in specific regions or towns. Their geographical origin determines quality and particular characteristics.

The Iblei were a people of ancient Sicily, renowned for the interpretation of dreams. A rainbow in Sicily is commonly called *Arcu di Noè* (Noah's Ark) or, depending on your mood, *Curuna do diavulu* (the devil's crown). If the color yellow prevails, a good year for wheat is forecast. When green prevails, it is a good year for olive oil. When red prevails, it will be a good year for wine.

coria

liqueurs

THere is no commercial production of liquor in the area. Some families make the following liqueurs, more to amuse themselves than out of need. These are recipes known as *della nonna* meaning "from my grandmother."

Elisir di rigulizia (Licorice Liqueur)

Ingredients
- 3/4 cup licorice root
- 8 ounces (1 cup) alcohol [pure, distilled]
- 2 teaspoons anise seeds
- Wild fennel leaves
- 1 1/2 cups sugar
- 24 ounces (3 cups) alcohol [pure, distilled]

Clean the root and smash it with a hammer until it is shredded. In a mixing bowl, let it infuse with 1 cup pure alcohol together with anise seeds. After 3 days, transfer to a pot and boil it with a little water and wild fennel leaves, reducing the liquid to about 1 cup. Add sugar, mixing thoroughly. After a week, strain the liquid to remove the herbs, add another 24 ounces of alcohol, and transfer to a clean bottle, hermetically seal, and shake occasionally.

This comes from the Arabic word *aliksir,* which means "philosopher's stone" or "long life medicine." Originally the term identified the magic matter that could transform everything into gold, or grant immortality. As it was impossible to find this substance, the name was passed on to a variously aromatized liqueur which, if it cannot give us immortality, will at least allow us to live the life granted to us in good cheer.

Rosolio di amarena (Black Cherry Liqueur)

It is difficult to obtain the exact ingredients and to describe the technique, such is the wide variety of these from family to family. But it is a very simple affair indeed. One puts approximately 2 pounds of bitter black cherries in a large bowl, removes the pits, crushes the remaining fruit, and adds the same weight of sugar (if you like it more bitter, add less sugar). Add 1 quart of pure, distilled alcohol to this, pour into a bottle and allow to infuse for a week, shaking the bottle often. After a week, filter this, and bottle and tightly seal the liqueur obtained. The cherries remaining, soaked in alcohol, can be eaten apart.

index of recipes

Lipari coast

FISH DISHES

Long-fin Tuna with Garlic
Sauce 40
  Alalònca cû l'agghiata

Stuffed Grilled Swordfish 41
  Braciulittini di pisci spata

"Drowned" Squid 42
  Calamari affucati

Mussel Soup 43
  Cozzi a bruoru

New Fish Soup 44
  Majatica a suppitèdda

Braised Silver Scabbard Fish or
Cutlassfish 45
  Mavestu, o spatula, in umitu

Swordfish Pie 46
  'Mpanata di pisci spata

Stockfish Messina-style 48
  Pisci stoccu a missinisa

Stockfish and
"Stuffed Bellies" 49
  *Pisci stoccu
  e ventri chini a ghiotta*

Raw Anchovies 88
  Anciova cruri

Roasted Garfish 89
  Augghi arrustuti

Roasted Stockfish 89
  Pisci stoccu arrustutu

Sand Lance, Catanese-style 90
  Cicireddu a catanisa

Buttoned-down "Bullet" Tuna 91
  Sangunusu abbuttunatu

Baccalà frittu 125

Tuna Semen 125
  Lattumi di tunnu

Poached Brill 126
  Rummu a stimpirata

Pickerel with Garlic 127
  Spicari all'agghiata

Angel Shark Marinara 128
  Squatru a matalotta

Fish Soup Siracusa-style 129
  Suppa a sirausana

River Trout with Catmint 130
  Trota du manghisi ccâ niputedda

Dogfish Pie 172
  'Mpanata di palummu

Sardines with Lettuce 173
  Sardi ccâ lattuca

Mullet 174
  Trigghiola

Tuna with Zucchini 175
  Tunnina ccâ cucuzza

VEGETABLES AND LEGUMES

CHEESE AND EGGS

Authentic ingredients as well as fresh, seasonal produce are essential for Italian cookery.
Here are selected companies providing Italian regional products. Check for their store
locations and mail order information.

A. G. Ferrari Foods	agferrari.com	877-878-2783
Balducci's	balduccis.com	800-225-3822
BuonItalia	buonitalia.com	212-633-9090
Citarella	citarella.com	212-874-0383
Corti Brothers	cortibros.biz	800-509-3663
Dean & DeLuca	deandeluca.com	800-221-7714
De Medici Importers	demedici.com	914-651-4400
Di Palo Fine Foods		212-226-1033
	gustiamo.com	718-860-2949
Manicaretti	manicaretti.com	888-952-4005
Todaro Brothers	todarobros.com	877-472-2764
Vivande Porta Via	vivande.com	415-346-4430
Zabar's	zabars.com	212-496-1234
Zingerman's	zingermans.com	888-636-8162

Of course, look to your local organic food shops and farmers markets for fresh, seasonal produce.

or grow your own!

Seeds from Italy	growitalian.com	781-721-5904